Births,
Deaths,
and Taxes

A. F. K. Organski
Jacek Kugler
J. Timothy Johnson
Youssef Cohen

Births, Deaths, and Taxes

The Demographic and Political Transitions

The University of Chicago Press
Chicago and London

A. F. K. Organski is professor of political science and program director of the
Center for Political Studies in the Institute for Social Research at the University of
Michigan. He is the author of several books and, with Jacek Kugler, wrote *The War
Ledger,* also published by the University of Chicago Press. Jacek Kugler is
associate professor of political science at Vanderbilt University. He is coauthor of
The War Ledger. J. Timothy Johnson is a sociologist and demographer for the
Program Evaluation Branch, Division of Reproductive Health, at the Centers for
Disease Control in Atlanta. Youssef Cohen is assistant professor of political
science at the University of Pennsylvania.

The University of Chicago Press, Chicago 60637
The University of Chicago Press, Ltd., London
© 1984 by The University of Chicago
All rights reserved. Published 1984
Printed in the United States of America
93 92 91 90 89 88 87 86 85 84 54321

Library of Congress Cataloging in Publication Data
Main entry under title:

Births, deaths, and taxes.

Includes bibliographical references and index.
1. Demography—Political aspects. 2. Fertility, Human—
Political aspects. 3. Mortality—Political aspects.
4. Taxation. I. Organski, A. F. K. 1923–
HB885.B47 1984   306'.2   83-17989
ISBN 0-226-63281-4
ISBN 0-226-63280-6 (pbk.)

Contents

Illustrations

Tables

Preface

There are obvious differences in the ways that
scholars who monitor societal behavior use demographic data. For demographers, demographic behavior is the variable to be explained. For
nondemographers, demographic structures and
behaviors—for example, age, sex, migration patterns,
fertility, and mortality—are factors to be used in
accounting for how collectivities behave. Students of
politics have overwhelmingly used demographic data in
this latter spirit. Political scientists routinely employ
demographic variables to help explain the political
behavior of national or subnational populations. This
book represents a break with that tradition in that it
uses politics to explain the movement observed in
fertility and mortality.

We pose the fundamental question, What effect do
the processes that have come to be known as "political
development" have on birthrates and death rates in
national populations? This connection has eluded rigorous and systematic analysis until now because there has
been no way of tracing the developmental pattern of
the political system in any rigorous and systematic
fashion. For the most part, few people have even
imagined that such a connection existed. For what links
could there be between the growing power of government and the reproductive behavior of the population
under its jurisdiction? But we have in fact found a very
important connection, and its implications are immense.

This book is the fruit of a collaboration between

three political scientists and a specialist in public health and population planning. Given its slimness and the number of authors, it seems proper to say who did what. It should be clear that each author contributed to every area of this work, and all together deserve equal praise and blame for the result. But collaboration, if efficient, implies division of labor. A. F. K. Organski took the lead in the theory, in the architecture of the book and in the writing. Jacek Kugler and Youssef Cohen contributed mightily to the theory and to the empirical analysis. J. Timothy Johnson led in preparing the demographic variables that formed the dependent side of the equation and made particularly valuable contributions in explaining the mysteries of demography. As a group, moreover, we owe a heavy debt to many colleagues. We are indebted to Dr. Ronald Freedman of the Center for Population Studies at the University of Michigan and Mr. Parker Mauldin of the Rockefeller Foundation for their intellectual support of this foray into the field of demography. We owe thanks to Dr. Christopher Braider and Mrs. Barbara Skala for their extensive editorial work; their comments helped us improve the final product. We also owe special thanks to six colleagues at the Center for Political Studies at the University of Michigan. Dr. Peter McDonough read the entire manuscript and made suggestions. Mr. Henry Heitowit proposed the title. Mr. Glenn Palmer and Mr. Samuel Evans made a herculean contribution to every phase of the data preparation and analysis. Dr. Ray Langsten helped us prepare the demographic data. Miss Deborah Eddy, with infinite patience and great skill, processed the manuscript through its many versions. We are also very grateful to the Defense Advanced Research Projects Agency for financial support for the broader project of which this work is a small part.

As always, none of those who helped are answerable for the use we made of their contributions. The responsibility for what has been written here is ours alone.

Introduction

In the following pages we shall ask a number of questions about the relation between *political change* and patterns of *fertility and mortality*. This link is a critical dimension of social, economic, and political development.

It has, of course, long been suspected that some such link exists,[1] but no one has yet properly explored it by empirical means. Worse still, the central proposition that, under conditions of development, political change and the extension of governmental control will directly and significantly shape demographic patterns in the same general way that socioeconomic development itself does has never been defined in a detailed and systematic manner or been subjected to thorough empirical testing. We have not, therefore, really understood what effect (if any) politics has on demographic systems. Still less do we understand how political change would bring about such an effect. It is to supply this want—to solve this dual problem of the existence and nature of the relation between politics and demography—that our efforts will primarily be directed.

We shall talk about such things as government and taxes, the cost of raising children, and what determines mortality rates—matters of perennial concern in the lives of individuals and nations alike. More to our present point, we believe they are all *related*. Government and taxes are positively related. The larger a government grows, the higher the level of taxation becomes; conversely, the less tax government manages to extract, the more restricted its size and the scope of its activity. But there is also a correlation between government's expansion and "vital rates": a correlation less accessible to empirical analysis than the first and inverse in character and direction.

We shall argue that the growth of government power, as measured by increases in taxation, finds real and direct expression, ceteris paribus, in the number of children born and the number of people dying in a given population. We have long suspected politics of playing a central role in patterned demographic change. Though this role has until recently eluded precise definition and quantitative assessment, it will indeed reveal itself as a crucial variable in the evolution of demographic systems. Its effect, we think, is correctly expressed in the following proposition: The larger the scale of government, the lower the rate of childbearing and the lower the rate of mortality.

Clearly, the relationships at issue here are far from trivial. Should empirical inquiry confirm that they are as we say, a new and potent determinant of the behavior of demographic systems will have yielded to analysis, and a series of important pieces in the giant puzzle of politics, population, development, and power will fall into place. Some questions of the highest significance in the field of development—the origins of population growth and decline, and the debate over whether the population problem can be solved by direct measures or whether, as some argue, the balance between population and resources can be redressed only by fundamental changes in society's structure—will take on fresh rigor and new meaning.

This research will, however, have a second, even more far-reaching result. To test our central hypothesis regarding the relation between politics and population, we have had to elaborate a method of estimating political development, a method that involved constructing an *index* capable of detecting and measuring such development. An accurate measure of political development would in itself be a significant advance, for political science has until recently entirely lacked a truly reliable instrument of this sort.[2] In the absence of such an instrument we have been unable to provide any genuinely systematic answers to a whole range of questions relating to the effectiveness of political systems. Just how efficient, for example, are the political institutions of the

United States or the Soviet Union, of China, Germany, or Japan? And how does the political performance of each of these states compare with that of the others? Were we to formulate a valid index of political development, the answers to questions like these, beyond the horizon of systematic political science research even a short while ago, would at last be within reach. We would equip ourselves to make comparisons of a kind previously unthinkable and to extend our knowledge of politics, and particularly of political relations between the great powers, into realms hitherto closed to us.

Thus our ultimate aim here is not simply to find an explanation for rates of birth and mortality in national populations; and our elaboration of a measure of political development, though first undertaken with this relatively narrow end in view, is no mere exercise in "index construction." Any successful attempt to measure political development and capacity, thereby making it possible to determine rigorously the differences in government effectiveness between rival political systems, is important and exciting in its own right. Our analysis of the effect of politics on vital rates may indeed be regarded as a test procedure validating our measures of the capacity of political systems. Many readers may in fact prefer to regard this aspect of the investigation as the main event and may see the defining of the role of political change on demographic behavior, interesting though it may seem, as no more than the laboratory exercise required to monitor the performance of the index of the capacity of political systems. In all cases where the connection between proposed measures and behaviors has not previously been tested, one is faced with the crucial question, How does one know these measures offer a valid index of the behaviors one claims they assess? Validity cannot be assumed. In reading this research, the reader can choose either angle of vision at no extra cost. In either case the procedure, the data, and the findings are exactly the same.

There are, moreover, sound theoretical reasons for thinking that a measure of the effects of political change on vital rates will prove an excellent test of how well political systems fulfill their basic responsibilities, thus supplying a peculiarly important means of gauging their viability. All political systems have two cardinal objectives. The first is to defend the nation at large against external threat; the other—the one we are principally concerned with in this book—is to arrange matters in such a way that domestic demands do not exceed available resources.

As regards the second function, there can be no question that a great deal of the pressure upon available resources stems from the number of people inhabiting the polity. The problem defines itself from this point of view, therefore, as one of regulating the size of the population in order to control demand. One obvious way of doing this is to control emigration and immigration—a direct means of regulating population employed by all governments. Another more indirect form of regulation is to constrain the pattern of reproduction itself. Reproductive behavior, of course, need not be constrained directly. Indeed, the most effective constraints are all indirect, bearing primarily on the enveloping contextual behaviors that themselves exert a direct influence on reproduction. For example, fertility rates may be influenced by the availability of housing, which in turn will be influenced by interest rates on mortgage money. They may also be influenced by public investment in education and by the pay women receive compared with what men earn for equal work. The list of such connections can be made long indeed. By throwing light on these surrounding areas that condition general forms of social behavior, analyzing how government influence is indirectly related to patterns of reproduction will yield an important insight into the role government plays in the daily existence of the governed population. For all these reasons, the connection between politics and vital rates has special meaning for students of politics.

Systemic Influences: Politics and Demographic Behavior

The relation between politics and the physical turnover of the population is part of the larger picture of how development unfolds, and it helps explain why some of us, Americans and others, have been lifted in the past 250 years into this brave new world we call developed.

The process of development can be thought of as a number of chain reactions running through the political, economic, social, and demographic structures of national societies. Such reactive chains vary in length; some have many links. For example, political change may alter the behavior of the economic system, giving rise to changes in modes of production or distribution that in turn find expression in new levels and patterns of urbanization that then modify the class structure of society and the belief systems of the masses and the elite. Some chains, on the other hand, contain as few as two links: change in the structure of the economy may induce change in political behavior, change in the political structure may precipitate change in the social structure, or change in the social structure may bring about changes in economic or political structures and go no further.

So far, changes in fertility and mortality have been accounted for as being the product of a long sequence of interactions between economic, social, psychological, and demographic variables. It has been argued, for instance, that in the European experience increases in the productivity of agriculture coupled with the appearance of industrial manufacturing sparked and sustained the growth of cities; that an associated improvement in the general standard of living led to a decrease in mortality; and that the concentration of the population in urban centers engendered a transformation in popular values reflected in the emergence of the "nuclear family." A schematic presentation of the process we have just described is presented below.

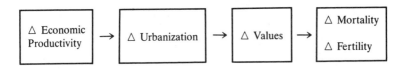

The sequence represented in the preceding schema is alleged to have unfolded very slowly, so that each set of changes had time to progress to a very considerable extent before the stimulus emanating from it finally sparked further transformations in other sectors of society. It is this fact, indeed, that suggests the strictly linear form of the schema. In contemporary development, however, where such changes take place much more rapidly and seem to occur almost simultaneously, the process leading to decreases in fertility and mortality would be more accurately represented as follows.

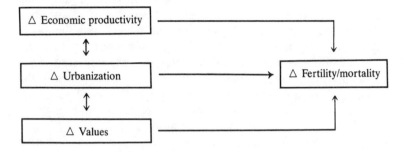

Whether the relations are schematically represented as linear or coordinate in form, the general underlying concept remains the same: increases or decreases in the rate of births and deaths are primarily the product of a complex of purely psychological and socioeconomic factors. But there is now a good deal of evidence tending to support the hypothesis that this does not tell the whole story and that a further two-link chain has somehow to be added: a chain in which change in political capacity resulting from the massive expansion and transformation of the political system under developmental conditions leads to dramatic decreases in the mortality and fertility of national populations.

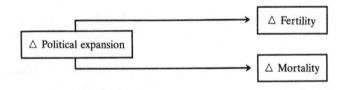

The need for this addition to previous ways of accounting for demographic behavior is illustrated by the following paradox. In the past two hundred years the developed portion of the world has experienced systematic reductions in fertility and mortality. Such declines have usually been interpreted as reflecting the transformation in popular attitudes and values consequent upon improved socioeconomic conditions and an increasingly urbanized way of life. But recently, major systematic reductions in the rate of population growth have occurred in countries like China, where the political system is very strong but social and economic changes have been insignificant and urbanization has progressed very little. Clearly, current models are not sufficient to explain this turn of events. Some other explanation must therefore be sought, and it is in this context that we advance the model proposed in this book, suggesting that *politics* plays a direct and potent part in demographic change and, more specifically, in the reduction of vital rates.

We should emphasize that we do not regard these alternative ways of accounting for the systematic reductions in population growth witnessed over the past two hundred years as mutually exclusive; we argue neither that politics alone nor that socioeconomic changes alone affect vital rates. Theoretically, both types of influences, whether in concert or separately, will reduce vital rates. We fully accept, moreover, that major social and economic development has generally been accompanied sooner or later by systematic decreases in the relative numbers of births and deaths observed in a given society. It is significant in our eyes, however, that one can find almost no cases where the socioeconomic change we call development has not been preceded by the institution of a solid state structure and the attendant massive transformation of the political system. On the other hand, there do exist cases today—contemporary China and North Vietnam, to mention only two—in which a very powerful political system has developed but socioeconomic changes have not yet begun in earnest. It is for this reason that we feel encouraged to assign to politics so decisive a role in determining demographic behavior.

Politics, Vital Rates, and Development

Here we shall pause to develop two crucial asides. The first concerns the true source of the interest of the discussions presented in these pages. For the problems we shall focus on here have to be placed in a wider perspective than that strictly appropriate to the question of demographic behavior itself, the point being that we discover in the relation between population and government growth an indispensable key to the comprehension of that general social, economic, and political metamorphosis, characteristic of the postindustrial world, that we have come to call national "development." The essential dynamics of the process of development are but imperfectly understood. There are, however, certain things we *do* know. We know that the mobilization of human and material resources we call socioeconomic development or modernization results from a number of concordant changes in the various sectors of society. The critical changes involved are higher productivity in the economic sector; a lowering of mortality and fertility in the demographic sector, eventually giving way to very modest increases in population; increasing urbanization in the social structure; the building up of a highly centralized state structure accompanied by a dramatic increase in the efficiency and reach of the political sector; and, finally, the increase in the presence of "modern" or "urban" or "instrumental" values among the national population.

Two differences between modern or postindustrial development and those partial increases in the mobilization of human and material resources observed in preindustrial societies stand out. First, in the "premodern" era, mobilization of material and human resources never advanced to so high a level, nor were its effects so rapid or permanent as they are today. Most important of all, however, before the modern era, mobilization or growth in one or, for that matter, more than one sector, when it occurred at all, did not provoke major, self-sustaining changes *in other sectors* of the life of the society. Development in the premodern era was essentially *paranemic*: even when change occurred in more than one sector, which we guess occurred rarely if at all, the various patterns of transformation unfolded side by side, without profound direct effects on one another. Political change, when it occurred, did not fundamentally alter the way the economy worked or the level of economic productivity. Nor did change in the economy alter the foundations of the social structure; and dramatic upheaval could take place in the economy, in the political structure, or even in the popular belief system without *permanently* changing the reproductive behavior of the population. For instance, the truly amazing transformations wrought in the political order of the ancient world by the Roman Empire did not alter, either for Romans or for the people under their sway, the mode of economic production, which remained subsistence agriculture; their own or their captives' demographic behavior; or the social structures in the various regions making up the metropolis or the empire. We can only speculate on the reasons for the imperviousness of the different sectors in premodern societies to changes in other sectors. We guess that this was a major reason for the comparative "stability" of the premodern world. It helps to explain why, repeatedly, when higher levels of mobilization were reached in the economy, for example, or in politics,[3] such increasing mobilization, finding no echo elsewhere, would begin to flag and then recede until at length everything returned to the status quo ante.

We think modern development is exactly the opposite in this respect. The processes of change in the different sectors do not run parallel to one another; they are instead *plectonemic* in character, that is, narrowly intertwined. Changes in the economy almost immediately spark changes in the political system or the social structure, and vice versa.[4] But though we may readily see how closely interwoven and interdependent these changes are in the contemporary world, it is the mechanisms that link them together, thus determining those chain reactions that carry the impulse for change from one sector to another, that are all-important to understand. In short, the "answers" to the questions of development are to be sought not in the nature of the changes themselves so much as in the nature of their *transmission*—that is, the links in the chain that carry changes from one sector of society into other sectors.

Looking at the question from this new point of view, it seems that the strength of the initial stimulus will be critical. If the stimulus proves weak, it will spark changes in another sector very slowly, if at all, whereas a powerful stimulus should set off a chain of reactions fairly quickly. Then again, the different sectors may well vary in their sensitivity to influences originating in other areas. The problem, then, would consist in determining where the strong stimuli come from and which sectors, offering the least resistance, will best transmit them. We would hazard the guess that the principal sources of change probably lie in the political, economic, and social structures and that demographic behavior and belief systems change as a consequence of changes in the socioeconomic and political spheres. Further, change in behavior may in fact precede changes in values. In short, demographic behavior and belief systems are in some sense the dependent and intermediate variables in development. One may also hazard the guess that the medium carrying the messages transmitting change are the cognitions, values, and beliefs of the populations.

The issue addressed in the preceding paragraphs goes to the heart of a question often posed in current writings: To what extent is the developmental process in underdeveloped and developing countries *today* comparable both in its outline and in its components to the developmental process in western European nations in the seventeenth, eighteenth, and nineteenth centuries?[5] It is usual to stress the dissimilarities between the beginnings of development in Europe and the developmental experience of countries today, and these are indeed many and profound. But taking care to respect such differences should not prevent us from making comparisons that might teach us more about developmental transformations then and now.

Be that as it may, the direct link between political change and vital rates is a critical joint in the whole structure of development, and it may well offer a clue to the way all other variables interact.

Which brings us to our second point, one with far-reaching implications regarding the future chances for economic development in the developing world today and, as a consequence of that development, regarding the distribution of power in the realm of international relations.

Consider. If the way we have accounted for demographic behavior in the past, linking increases and decreases in vital rates exclusively to social and economic factors, provides the only correct explanation, then the developing world is in for far more trouble in the future than even the bleak history of the past few decades would indicate.[6]

The reasons for this are not hard to understand. In subsystem economics, levels of savings and productivity and levels of population growth are inversely related: more of one, less of the other. Economic advancement requires savings and the transformation of savings into capital: when all is said and done, savings are the indispensable fuel for the development of economies, because without savings there is no investment. Subsistence economies can provide savings only with the greatest difficulty. Nor can they easily increase production, because their productivity is very low and difficult to change. They cannot decrease consumption by decreasing the existing standard of living because their populations are already living at subsistence levels. They can in principle lighten the task of saving by decreasing the number of people for which their societies must provide. Given the chronic underemployment in subsistence agricultures, reducing "surplus" population need not affect production levels. At the same time, a decline in population would curb demand, thus improving the chances of accumulating the capital base required for investment and growth. But how is that to be brought about when uncontrolled population growth throws major impediments in the way of economic expansion and when social and economic underdevelopment in turn encourages a psychology conducive to high rates of population growth?

In the orthodox view of the way the system works, then, the developing world seems to be caught in a vicious circle from which, according to the model of development now in use, there can be no lasting escape. Thus all hope of modernization will prove an illusion: one third of humanity, already barely at subsistence level, faces ever increasing pauperization, doomed to sink ever deeper in the mire of impoverishment, overpopulation, and powerlessness.[7]

But what if, instead, as the model presented and discussed in this book suggests, changes in the political structure influence demographic trends and, further, the expansion of the political system in fact brings down birth and death rates regardless of changes in productivity or the degree of urbanization observed in a given society? In this case the chances of economic growth in underdeveloped nations are much brighter, at least for those countries that have already succeeded in establishing effective governments. For the key would no longer lie in an accumulation of capital and an increase in productivity that are beyond their grasp by reason of uncontrollable population growth; it would lie in the emergence of a solid state structure—something that, as the examples of China and North Vietnam show, is essentially independent of social, economic, and demographic factors.

If the relation between the political and demographic behavior of national systems is in fact as we say—if there is indeed a close link between the political and demographic behavior of national systems and if the growth of the political system affects demographic trends—then those nations in the developing world that, despite stagnating development in the economic sector, nevertheless already possess powerful and effective governments are much more likely to enjoy economic development. The corollary to this proposition, of course, is that economically underdeveloped countries that fail to evolve *effective political systems* will continue to fall behind economically and will remain at the bottom of the international ladder. Should our hypothesis prove wrong, however —if the changes in political structure we think so important have no direct influence tending to reduce fertility and mortality—then, as currently believed, the decrease in vital rates indispensable to development can be brought about only by social, psychological, and economic factors. And this in turn will mean that even those countries in the developing world that have in fact managed to establish effective governments are unlikely to develop economically. They will instead, like all other nondeveloped societies, face increasing pauperization and, eventually, even an increasing erosion of their newly acquired political capacity itself.

Yet what is at stake here is not merely the fate of individual nations but the whole network of international relations. The failure to realize significant economic progress clearly leaves the nations of the developing world at a distinct disadvantage in their dealings with developed nations: economic stagnation at home leads directly to political powerlessness on the international scene. On the other hand, if—and it is a big "if"—growth in the effectiveness of political systems can truly bring down vital rates, such nations can buy precious time in which to start economic growth. And if countries manage to develop economically, they will also, at the same time, make major gains in power at the international level: the potent combination of a well-organized political structure, high productivity, and a favorable ratio of dependent to productive populations will propel them up the ladder of influence in international affairs. There can be little doubt that the structure of the distribution of international power forty or fifty years from now rides largely on whether political development does or does not have the effect of bringing down vital rates. If it has no effect on them, then the gap between the haves and the have-nots of this world, where it does not widen, should remain fundamentally the same. But if it does have the effect we believe it to have, then the geopolitical landscape of the future will change radically and forever.[8]

Goverment Policies and Demographic Behavior

Throughout this book we shall be concerned with the effects that the enormous expansion and structural change observed in developing political systems have on fertility and mortality. But it should be clear that such effects, if any, will be unintended. Though by expanding governments may indeed affect the reproductive behavior and mortality of the populations under their control, the changes they bring about in this way are unconscious; they make them without trying to. But can governments deliberately reshape demographic trends? We take it for granted that, at least where death rates are concerned, they can. Fertility, on the other hand, is something else again. Can government policy be effective in this field? It is an important question.

The history of the twentieth century is full of examples of governments' trying to regulate increases and decreases in the size of the populations under their authority. Over the past twenty years, for instance, as everyone knows, governments in the developing world have made herculean efforts to stem explosive population growth, promoting reductions in fertility by instituting birth control programs, by distributing contraceptive devices, by facilitating abortions, and on occasion even by resorting to enforced sterilization. In contrast, in the thirties, frightened by what they thought was an ominous trend toward rates of birth only slightly above, or even below, those required to balance the mortality rate—a trend threatening the very existence of their states—certain European governments undertook to raise the level of fertility by prohibiting abortion and the use of contraception and by providing "incentives" in the form of better housing, tax privileges, and the creation of day-care centers designed to encourage people to have more children. Nor is the trend toward depopulation behind us. Thus certain Eastern European governments today, notably those of East Germany and Czechoslovakia, disturbed, it seems, by birthrates that have dropped sufficiently to produce an actual decrease in population, have anticipated the worst and taken measures to stimulate childbearing.

The reasons policymakers give for intervening are many, including the health or welfare of the population, the enhancement of national power, the pursuit of economic development, and so on.[9] But there are even deeper reasons. Commenting on plunging birthrates in Sweden in a book published in the United States in 1941, Alva Myrdal presented the case for her government's intervention to redress the demographic balance in her country this way:

> Population constancy was felt by the average citizen to be an end or a value in itself. This direct valuation, a feeling of national self-pity at the prospect of death and a pride in the collectivity of the national culture, was presented in various forms. Its common minimum basis was an attitude that "our society is too good not to be preserved." . . . It is not going to be so stimulating to work for a national culture that is under liquidation. It is not going to be so satisfying to build up a social structure which our children are not going to inherit.[10]

One may well wonder about the feelings Dr. Myrdal ascribes to the "average citizen": the argument she puts forward seems to express the wishes and preoccupations of the elite rather than the anxiety of the masses about their own and their neighbors' reproductive habits. Be that as it may, the essential motive inducing governments to involve themselves in such matters comes down to this. The foundation of a nation's wealth and influence is its people, for it is people who work and people who fight; they are the ultimate resource at the state's disposal, its most precious asset. It is, then, hardly surprising that governments should take an active interest in preserving the quality of this resource, trying to either increase or to decrease the size of the populations under their control, depending on the circumstances.

The question regarding population policy is as follows: When governments become concerned over demographic trends and try to redirect them, does what they do make any difference? And if it does, what kind of difference does it make? Or again, Under what conditions do government efforts at redirecting demographic trends make the sort of difference the government is looking for? Obviously, the conclusions we reach on this score will depend on our expectations concerning the efficacy of government action. The question may be put another way: What outcomes may we reasonably expect from government action in the area of population?

We shall, however, turn our attention to population policy only at the very end of the book, and even then only briefly. Nor shall we give any answers. There can be no question that matters of policy are the logical next step in exploring the consequences of expanding political systems from the point of view of demographic behavior, consequences forming the main burden of the following discussions. Still, policy is very different from the sort of thing we wish to examine here. Government policies represent a conscious and deliberate effort on the part of constituted authorities, carried out in the name of the nation as a whole, to bring about certain well-defined changes. But while the efforts a government makes to influence vital rates constitute "a manipulable," something over which it has direct control, the effect of the dramatic expansion of the political system under conditions of development does not. Thus, to the extent that the issues reviewed here turn on the unintended and unmanipulable effects political systems exert on vital rates at different levels of political development, the question of population policy has no direct bearing on our argument. The questions we shall raise in this connection at the end of the book will therefore mainly represent a research agenda.

Plan of the Book

Our first chapter will introduce in broad outline the concept of the demographic transition. This theory, once thought of as the most important theoretical statement in the field of demography, has lost a good deal of support among demographers. We shall therefore discuss the flaws revealed in the demographic transition theory by recent research. This discussion will lead us to suggest certain revisions of the original theory, after which we shall present the reasons why we think that including such new elements in any model of demographic behavior under conditions of development should improve our ability to account for demographic trends. The second chapter will present the theory behind the model we ourselves present, how in fact we think state making and the expansion of the political system affect vital rates. This second chapter will contain a description of the forces pushing for the development of the political system and present the theory behind the method used to measure overall progress in state making. The third chapter will expose in detail the way we made operational the model of state growth described in chapter 2. Our fourth chapter will be given over to the analysis constituting the experiment by which we tested our hypotheses, and to a description of our findings. This is followed by a brief review of all we have done and an epilogue raising some questions that go beyond the data reported in this book. It is in this very last part of the book that we shall discuss issues of government population policy.

Now let us turn to a review of the principal features of the model scholars have used in accounting for the behavior of vital rates.

1 The Demographic Transition

The Theory

We begin with demographic theory.

Variations in the rates of mortality and fertility experienced by national populations in the course of development have largely been accounted for by exclusive reference to socioeconomic and demographic factors. It was Frank Notestein who first brought the massive demographic, economic, and social transformations into an orderly and meaningful relation with each other in his "theory of the demographic transition." It may be helpful, then, to begin by examining some of the principal components of Notestein's model[1] and some of the more salient objections raised in the many debates the theory has inspired since it first appeared more than fifty years ago. What we will present here is no more than a general sketch or outline of the model of the demographic transition: there will be no details, merely an overview of what the model tells us. Our reasons for not going beyond a general description are simple. To specialists in demography, the model is well known. At one time, some fifteen years ago, it was still considered the major large-scale theoretical construct in the field. To nondemographers, the only thing of interest is the general gist of what the theory of the demographic transition has to say about demographic behavior and the main arguments regarding how well the theory has predicted the demographic behavior of national populations. For our purposes here the important thing is the general outline of the process held to lie at the core of the demographic transition. What we need to match with the process of the growth of political systems in order to see what effect politics exerts on vital rates is simply the general process of socioeconomic and demographic change and nothing more. The reader desiring more detail may consult the vast scientific literature on the subject, and summaries of this literature will be found in semiscientific journals specifically designed for the knowledgeable nonspecialist.[2]

Notestein argued that the economic and social transformations we have come to call "national development" are the major sources of the profound changes in the demographic behavior of national populations observed since the turn of the eighteenth century. During this process, countries moved from the high birth and death rates (the stage of "high potential growth") characteristically associated with economic and social underdevelopment to the low birth and death rates of economically and socially developed populations (the stage of "incipient decline")—up to now the position attained only by European countries, by some of the countries settled by Europeans overseas, and by Japan. During an intermediary stage, that of "transitional growth," both birth and death rates fell, but the latter more rapidly than the former, causing a massive increase in population.[3]

The nomenclature of the demographic transition model is selfexplanatory. The first stage is called one of "potential growth" because, during the process by which underdeveloped nations, in which both birth and death rates are high, gradually realize the social and economic gains necessary for development, mortality is expected to be brought under control well in advance of any permanent decline in fertility. This creates the conditions for an inevitable explosive rise in population in the next stage. Thus the rapid increase in population experienced in Europe during the eighteenth and nineteenth centuries is held to have been the result of a dramatic reduction in the death rate rather than an increase in rates of births, which were already high in any case. The population explosion that began in much of the world immediately after World War II was also the result of a dramatic reduction in mortality. During this initial phase, however, population growth remains strictly potential, since it has still to await the decline in mortality brought about by socioeconomic development.

Stage 2 is said to be one of "transitional growth" because it marks the passage from one form of demographic equilibrium, characteristic of stage 1, to another that is characteristic of fully developed nations. During this intermediary phase, a progressive movement of population toward urban centers, the emergence of secondary production, and higher productivity in the economic sector lead to improvements in living conditions sufficient to achieve a significant reduction in mortality rates. As a result, the potential growth of stage 1 is now realized, and population increases very rapidly for a time. However, socioeconomic factors are by now at work leading to the gradual formation of new urban values that in turn promote a decline in fertility. Accordingly, birthrates subsequently begin to drop rapidly, but only following the already low death rates.

In stage 3, finally, the trends established in the preceding phases pursue their course. Birthrates are now low, close to the very low death rates, and the demographic structure is again in balance. The danger is, of course, that, if birthrates continue to decline as they are expected to do under the theory of the demographic transition, negative growth will result. For this reason stage 3 is called one of "incipient decline."

An *idealized* version of the demographic transition is set forth in figure 1. As the figure shows, in stages 1 and 3 vital rates are roughly in balance and, as a result, the natural rate of increase is low.[4] In stage 2, on the other hand, death rates are much lower and falling while births are still high, though these too are slowly beginning to come down: consequently, the natural rate of increase is very large. This, incidentally, is the stage of the demographic transition that is of central interest to this study.

Under the demographic transition theory, then, the mainspring

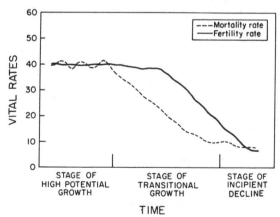

Fig. 1. An idealized scheme of the demographic transition.

of change in rates of fertility and mortality is psychosocial and economic change, also a major component in national development. Why growth in economic productivity and an increasingly urbanized way of life, the phenomena at the root of socioeconomic development, should cause the sequential decline in birth and death rates was not hard to explain. Death from starvation and disease owing to scarcity, poor sanitation, and inadequate shelter had for millennia plagued populations entirely dependent on subsistence agriculture. The increased economic productivity brought about by mechanized manufacture and the hitherto unimaginable wealth that came in its wake, coupled with the greater availability of food achieved by improvements in agricultural productivity and transportation and with the improved sanitation associated after a time with urban life, raised standards of living. As a result, death rates plummeted. Acting in combination with the new and peculiar pressures of life in cities, on the other hand, economic development and the shift to urban values, promoting an eventual shift to "nuclear" family patterns, produced a drop in fertility rates. That there should have been a delay in these decreases in birthrates was alleged to have been due to the resistance to the new urban values and modes of behavior posed by the village mentality of a population only recently transplanted to the cities.[5]

One of the major consequences of the transition undergone by the demographic structure is a fundamental redistribution of the population among the various age groups. Redistributions of this kind are of vital importance to economic development and national power, for the change in age structure that accompanies the passage from a "traditional" to a "modern" social system brings additional manpower both to the economy and to the state for government use. The age pyramids shown in figure 2 for three countries at three stages of demographic and economic development tell the story at a glance. The most developed countries are found to enjoy the most favorable proportion of potential workers to dependent population. Not only are these the most productive countries, but they are also the societies least burdened by dependents and possessing the greatest number of people able to work and fight.[6] The connection between power, wealth, and numbers should, then, be plain.

But the concept of the demographic transition has been the

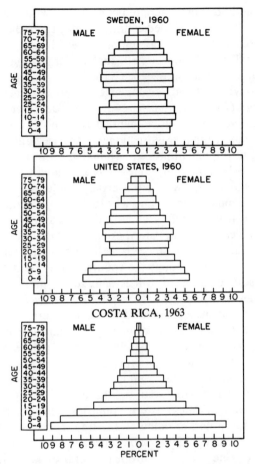

Fig. 2. Age distribution and the demographic transition. From United Nations, *Demographic Yearbook,* 1964 and 1961, table 5.

object of criticism, and it is important to present, at least in a very general way, what this criticism has been. One major potential weakness of the demographic transition concept stems from the fact that its authors constructed a dynamic model out of cross-sectional data: they had, in other words, to reconstruct the evolution from underdevelopment to development using information relating to various isolated "moments" in that evolution. This procedure is, of course, often unavoidable, given the chronic lack of data series of the requisite length. Faced with a situation of this kind, the method usually adopted consists of taking advantage of the fact that highly developed countries today share the same slice of time with countries developing fairly quickly and a number of countries still quite undeveloped, that is, largely rural societies living in large part on subsistence agriculture. One then *assumes* that underdeveloped and developing countries are tracing in their own demographic evolution the course that developed countries have already followed before them. It is in this fashion that one transforms data from a cross-sectional, static view into a dynamic view of the development process. Though this procedure is, as we have said, well established, it clearly is a decidedly risky business enfolding two perhaps wholly unwarranted inferential leaps.

In the first place, there is no way to know for certain that the data derived from currently underdeveloped and developing nations reproduce the historical experience of the developed societies under study. Second, there is as little certainty that, in their own demographic evolution, the countries at present engaged in the process of development will actually follow in the footsteps of the countries that have already achieved high levels of economic productivity and urbanization. One cannot therefore determine whether the theory of the demographic transition presents an accurate description of the historical demographic experience of today's developed countries; nor, just as important, can one determine whether the theory affords an accurate prediction of the course that will be followed by those African, Asian, Latin American, and Middle Eastern countries that illustrate demographic trends at earlier points of the trajectory toward development. Is the current demographic behavior of underdeveloped societies the same as that of European countries before industrialization? Is the experience of societies actively engaged in the process of development similar, at least in general outline, to the demographic experience of today's developed societies before they reached a similar level of modernization? Will the present developing countries reproduce in the future the same demographic patterns currently witnessed among the nations of the developed world? One cannot *know*. But the issue is clear: were the answers to these questions other than an unqualified yes, then the theory of the demographic transition could not claim to be more than a simple description of vital rates observed in societies in the underdeveloped, developing, and developed worlds at the time of its presentation. It is clear that its author(s) did not share this view.

Be that as it may, observers began to note even more worrisome problems. As more information became available on the behavior of vital rates in the developing and developed worlds today and in preindustrial Europe, the data seemed in many cases to contradict the expectations engendered by the theory of the demographic transition.

First of all, birthrates in countries currently in the stage of transitional growth do not behave as one might think they would in accordance with the demographic transition concept. It certainly seemed for a long time as though the European demographic experience was not to be repeated, that birthrates were not to come down after plunging death rates. A yawning gap opened between birth and death rates—death rates plummeted while fertility did not—and developing countries posted staggering population increases. And there seemed to be no end to the process. Fertility in developing countries remained high in the 1950s and continued so in the 1960s. Even at the beginning of the seventies there seemed to be no relief in sight. Was this frighteningly explosive growth in population really transitional? Was it going to stop? When would one see signs of deceleration? These seemed, at the time, unanswerable questions.[7] It was only toward the end of the seventies that widely credited evidence began to accumulate indicating that rates of population growth were beginning to slacken.

Other questions about the validity of the theory of the demographic transition centered on the theory's prediction of the behavior of vital rates in the third stage, that is, at a point when nations have reached economically developed levels. The theory had argued that the decrease in population growth observed in so many Western European countries in the 1930s could be expected to continue in the postwar period, that a population decline was the fate of all already developed countries in the decades ahead, and that other countries, still perched on lower rungs of the developmental ladder, would face the same kind of demographic future as they developed. But, of course, for the next three decades this projection failed to come true. In the fifties and sixties, some highly developed countries grew faster than countries trailing far behind them. The population of the United States, for example, grew faster than that of Spain or Italy. In the developed world, birthrates rose and death rates fell further and faster than expected, owing in part to the larger proportion of young people of childbearing age in their populations as well as to advances in medicine that lengthened the lives of the old.[8] Again, it was not until the seventies that it became clear that, in the developed world, birthrates were plunging to match the very low death rates.

Nor did the postulated behavior of vital rates in the stage of high potential growth seem to mirror the demographic behavior of Northwestern European countries in their preindustrial period. Hard data on that period were not available when the theory was first proposed. Subsequent research, however, indicates that, in preindustrial Europe, birth and death rates were not *uniformly* high. A good deal of variation seems to have been present not only from one country to another, but also in different regions in the same country and even—at first glance most puzzling of all—in different localities within the same region. Nor were fertility and mortality rates at the national levels stable over time: massive fluctuations occurred, sometimes almost as profound as the decreases that the model specified would take place as the result of the transition from one phase in the process of development to another. Witness the behavior of vital rates in England between

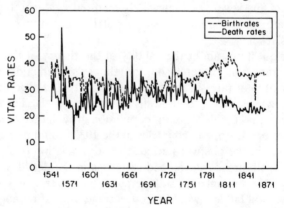

Fig. 3.   Crude birth and death rates in England, 1541–1871. From E. A. Wrigley and R. S. Schofield, *The Population History of England, 1541–1871: A Reconstruction* (Cambridge: Harvard University Press, 1981), table A3.3, pp. 531–35.

1541 and 1871 (see fig. 3). The most worrisome part of all was perhaps that what evidence there was, and admittedly such evidence was not plentiful, indicated that some fundamental relations postulated by the theory of the demographic transition seemed to be contradicted at many points in the historical record of the demographic behavior of European countries for which data were available. This was also true of the demographic behavior of populations in the currently developing portion of the world. Once one went beyond the very aggregate level of analysis, many of the links between mortality and fertility stipulated by the demographic transition theory did not seem to hold: decreases in birthrates preceded decreases in death rates, birthrates fell before economic development began, and in some cases rural populations posted decreased birthrates before decreases in birthrates were recorded in cities.[9]

Exceptions played havoc with expectations. Given such cause for criticism, how useful can the demographic transition theory be? As one would expect, there is disagreement on this score. Some specialists in the field still believe; some do not: Some believe with reservations. The following views give the reader a glimpse of the division of opinion.

Paul Demeny writes:

> Modern demography is above all, about demographic transition. . . . there is description in the spirit of the narrow, literal definition of demography—a description of quantitative aspects of human populations. . . . On a more ambitious level there is the task of explanation. . . . Why did fertility (mortality) start to decline when it did? Why was the decline faster here than it was elsewhere?. . . . It is hoped that the answers to these questions will eventually jell into a *theory* of demographic transition: a set of generalizations which are capable of explaining the onset, the course, and the final outcome of past demographic transitions, and which will also give us the key to the prediction of transitions yet to come.[10]

Here is the view of Nathan Keyfitz.

> Development seems sooner or later to have brought a reduction of population growth in all instances where it has

occurred. . . .the correlation is not perfect, but still history seems to be saying, that with more or less lag, industrialization has led to reduced family size.[11]

A more extensive statement of what the "scientific community" believed were the limitations of the theory of the demographic transition was presented by Michael Teitelbaum:

popular adoption of a scientific theory usually lags far behind the elaboration of the theory itself. The theory of the demographic transition was originally developed nearly a half century ago, and ironically its explanatory and predictive power has come to increasing scientific doubt at the very time that it is achieving its greatest acceptance by non scientists. In scientific circles, only modest claims are now made for transition theory as an explanation of the very demographic experiences from which the theory was originally drawn—those of 19th century Europe. When applied to the markedly different social and economic circumstances of modern day Asia, Africa, and Latin America, the explanatory and predictive power of transition theory is open to further scientific question.

the theory of the demographic transition *is essentially a plausible description* of complex social and economic phenomena which took place in 19th century Europe. It is notably lacking in such components of theories as a specifiable and measurable mechanism of "causation" and a definite time scale. It has, however, generated some very general hypotheses which have been affirmed by subsequent events, for example, the proposition that mortality generally responds more quickly than fertility to the forces of medicine and development, and the prediction of the 1950s that regions such as Asia could therefore be expected to experience large population increases in the decades following. (italics added)[12]

Two points should be made. First, the statements above are not mutually exclusive. One can agree with the criticisms that the theory of the demographic transition lacks "a specifiable and measurable mechanism of 'causation' and a definite time scale." Thus there is no way to know when the inflection points in the curves traced by vital rates will occur, how smooth the trajectories in question will be, and so on and on. Had the authors of the model been able to provide all that, clearly we would be much further on the road to understanding demographic behavior and development than we are at present. Given the record, then, one must certainly agree with Keyfitz that there is no perfect correlation between demographic behavior and socioeconomic change. But at the same time one can also agree with the judgment of Paul Demeny that "Modern demography is above all, about demographic transition." Indeed, that statement can be considered a point of departure for the work presented in this book.

In a word, the correlation between "development" and the movement of vital rates is not perfect—which brings us to our second point. We suggest that one source of the imperfection is that the description of "development" has, as a general rule, included only social and economic variables. It will be improved, we believe, if one takes political variables into account. We should also note in passing that much of the criticism of the demographic transition model has been directed at stages 1 (high potential growth) and 3 (incipient decline) and that most of the problems dealt with in this book are concerned with the process described in stage 2 (transitional growth) of the demographic transition. This is a segment in nations' lives when mortality is falling further and faster than the decrease in fertility, bringing about a massive demographic transformation. It is usually during this period that political development, like economic development, is at its most pronounced and is easiest to detect.

A Flaw in the Model: Political Development— The Omitted Factor

We have already suggested that the demographic transition theory, as originally formulated, provides a general guide to the way demographic trends evolve under *conditions of development*, but that all explanations of the behavior of vital rates have, to date, omitted the effects exerted on birth and death rates by the massive expansion of the state and the political system that also takes place under conditions of development. As we shall show, such effects are as important in this regard as the restructuring of the economy and social life itself.

Political Expansion and Death Rates

Let us briefly review the reasons for thinking that political change is an important factor in producing the downward trend in vital rates associated with national development. To begin with death rates, it seems reasonable to suggest that, in the "premodern" world, the absence of central state power will give rise to high levels of insecurity and encourage the violence and disorder endemic in the nondeveloped world, which will in turn have important primary and secondary consequences for the behavior of vital rates. For not only do people die as a result of constant fighting, but the conditions of social disorder make it difficult to tend the fields, set aside surplus food against times of want, transport this food to places where famine has broken out, and isolate places in which epidemics have occurred, all essential to keeping mortality rates down.

It will be readily understood, then, that the development of central political control will inevitably make a great deal of difference so far as mortality is concerned. For it should be noted that even the very minimal growth in the capacity of the political system that accompanied the state-building process in Europe in past centuries and, of course, the state-building efforts and the consequent centralization of power in developing systems today means, after an initial period of turbulence, the imposition of some modicum of peace and order throughout the country: It means the slow eradication of fighting and the depredations of local lords and bandits, more effective protection from external aggression, more effective maintenance of basic communications, and the introduction of at least rudimentary sanitary facilities. And at the same time as these actions help lay the foundations for a growing state structure, they also bring about a sharp decrease in death rates.

The connection between political growth and mortality is particularly telling in the developing world today, because as they increase in effectiveness the governments of developing nations can take advantage of advanced medical and sanitary technologies unavailable in preindustrial Europe when medical knowledge was still primitive. Indeed, so dramatic has been the fall of death rates, despite the delays in socioeconomic development itself, that the balance between births and deaths has been destroyed. It is also interesting to note in this connection that, largely owing to medicine and sanitation, developing countries have managed to lower death rates despite the fact that, as we shall see below, the costs of expansion at the beginning of the transformation of the political sector are very high. Be that as it may, it seems very reasonable to argue on theoretical grounds that strengthening the political system in societies living at or immediately above subsistence levels does in reality affect death rates.

It has of course been argued ever since World War II that a primary cause of the decline of death rates realized in the developing world was simply that the new nations borrowed the sanitary and medical practices of the West. This, of course, is quite correct, but it is also misleading. The fact is that developing countries have made a major contribution of their own to preserving their people's lives. European medical and sanitary practices could not have been grafted onto underdeveloped societies without at least a minimally effective political system. Rickety and uncertain though the political systems in the underdeveloped world may well be, they have performed well enough in providing sanitary and medical facilities, systems of communication, investment in the economic infrastructure, and so on, factors universally credited with the sharp drop in death rates and the saving of hundreds of millions of lives. Borrowings from the West, like economic and social changes, are only part of the answer. The importance of the contribution the evolving political system makes should not be underestimated.

Political Expansion and Birthrates

Let us now turn to birthrates. From the point of view of our understanding of the mechanisms governing the evolution of demographic systems, the importance of the impact of political expansion on mortality rates pales in comparison with the importance of its effect on rates of birth. But, once again, what reason is there for thinking that the massive restructuring and growth of the political system during development influence the reproductive behavior of the population? Aside from the effects of government-sponsored birth control or family-planning programs, what significant connection could there possibly be between political change and fertility? But ask yourself, What exactly does the growth of the political system mean? Whatever else it may mean, it must entail penetration by the central governing elite into successive layers of the national society and the reorganization of people's lives. And how could such a massive government intrusion in people's lives fail to affect their reproductive behavior?

Consider. Governments interfere with the traditional ordering of family life. First, as nations develop, governments have almost invariably raised both the direct and the indirect social, economic, and psychic costs of having children by restricting child labor, expanding compulsory education, increasing child health care, and protecting the rights of children even against their parents. Moreover, government power has been used to defend the rights of women, to give them the opportunity to work and seek an education, to inherit property, initiate divorce, receive child support, and so on. Governments have also raised the marriage age and eased restrictions on the knowledge and use of methods and materials to postpone pregnancies or even terminate them altogether. Nor is even this list exhaustive. How can government actions of this kind help but directly and indirectly affect the reproductive behavior of the population? It all comes down to this: governments have increased the costs of bearing and rearing children and have also made parents more and more aware of the price. True, this was not in most cases their intention: hardly any of the government measures we have mentioned were expressly aimed at regulating reproductive behavior. But the fact remains that the unintended consequences of government action have had the effect of seriously braking birthrates even when quite different goals were in view.

It is incredible that the importance of change and growth in the political system should have been overlooked so completely until now, though perhaps "overlooked completely" is too strong a way of putting it. There has before now been considerable awareness that other determinants of fertility exist apart from the ones usually considered. For example, Geoffrey McNicoll laments "that we have somehow not yet discovered or devised appropriate parameters of the fertility decision-making environment

—parameters that would reduce unmanageable complexity to a semblance of order."[13] He suggested that one ought to explore the effects of institutional factors. Similar suggestions that political factors were operating in the background by creating conditions that led to reductions in vital rates can also be found in some discussions of the demographic transition.[14] Again, there has been at least one recent attempt to relate political change to fertility. The interpretation of the phenomenon differs radically from the one proposed here, and no empirical evidence was furnished in its defense. Still, this other hypothesis should be presented here at least in broad outline.

The researchers in question were concerned with the demographic experience of Western Europe, and the proposition they advanced is that the decrease in vital rates in Europe reflected Western Europeans' desire to obtain greater control over their own lives. The "political evidence" adduced in support of this contention is that Europeans have in the past fought the tyrannies of their kings to gain greater personal liberty. Was it not possible, then, that this same thirst for individual liberty carried over into the private lives of people and therefore also lies behind reduced European fertility?

The argument is ingenious. It is perhaps best to let the authors summarize their own hypothesis: "One must admit that this is very persuasive. If man rebels against the total power of the church and of the state, it is because he wishes to affirm his control over his own life . . . responsible man takes control over his own reproduction and submits it to his rational decision."[15] This psychopolitical interpretation, as we may call it, should be particularly attractive to researchers interested in belief systems and the effects of beliefs, values, and attitudes on social, economic, and political behavior. And, of course, the general approach, if not the specific proposition, does seem on the whole to indicate the right way to go. In the final analysis, when attempting to explain human behavior one must always provide a psychological component. How do the men and women in question *perceive* the problem, and how does this perception motivate their actions? Moreover, the wish to control one's own existence, husband one's own resources, and channel them in the direction one wishes is the prime motive for limiting the size of families.

Whether such *psychopolitical motives* have actually been responsible for lowering birthrates in Western Europe remains open to question, however. The hypothesis is definitely appealing and enjoys a certain surface plausibility, but in our view it is not ultimately persuasive. In the first place, it should be clear that the kinds of motives, beliefs, and behavior involved in the fight against political tyranny are very different from the motives, beliefs, and behavior involved in resisting the even more oppressive tyranny of a large and often unwanted progeny one cannot really support. It should be remembered, furthermore, that the segments of the population who fight against or object to political tyranny are not necessarily the same as those who lower their fertility. There are, besides, too many examples of European and non-European populations in which birthrates have fallen under the worst of tyrannies to accept totally this proposition in regard to the reduction in Western European fertility. Think of the European Russians under communism and the Chinese in the People's Republic. There are, further, a number of obvious examples of populations, such as those of India and Bangladesh since independence, that have in fact fought themselves free of the tyrannies of indigenous and foreign masters while retaining very high levels of fertility.

In any event, we think it is sounder to argue the opposite thesis. We know that fertility is extremely responsive to societal pressures. If economic conditions are poor or wages fall, if work is hard to come by or the price of food goes up, fertility tends to drop, whereas if economic conditions improve, fertility tends to rise. It seems plausible to suppose that, when political conditions are harsh, governments use their muscle to manipulate individual lives and restructure the conditions under which the communities must live, using such measures as drafting young people into military service, relocating centers of employment, providing education, and, through heavy taxation, devouring the resources available for the necessities of life. People will respond to such pressures, as they invariably do to harsh conditions, by cutting down on the number of children they have.

The difference in the angles of vision we have presented is important. In developing countries, at least, declining birthrates do not, then, reflect the fact that men and women wish to control their own destinies and fight for freedom of choice either in their private lives or as collectivities. The reality appears to us far less uplifting and far more drab and commonplace. Particularly in the case of mass populations, European or non-European, it seems more plausible to argue that they respond in any way and to the extent they can to the material realities to which they are captive: if they cannot afford children because there are not enough resources for everyone to survive, they do not have them, or they have fewer of them than they would otherwise have had. In short, they adapt to the crushing pressures exerted by the expanding state, and such pressures are equally heavy regardless of whether the form of the government is autocratic, democratic, or totalitarian.

Political Expansion: The Sequence in the Fall of Births and Deaths

There is an order followed by decreases in the numbers of births and deaths that deserves note. The demographic transition theory leads one to expect that death rates will fall sooner than birthrates. And we also believe that political growth should bring death rates down further and sooner than birthrates. The reasons for this order as set forth in the demographic transition theory have been amply discussed elsewhere and need not be repeated. The main reason why political development should have the same effect, on the other hand, should be mentioned here and can be simply stated as follows.

Even modest increases in governmental capacity will generate downward pressure on mortality rates. The reduction of internal violence and instability not only saves lives directly and immediately, but affects activities in turn directly related to sustaining life. The protection of people's lives is so fundamental, a value so widely shared by all members of society, that governments will make every sacrifice to achieve it. And because of this widespread consensus, governmental policies aimed at decreasing mortality rates are very likely to meet with less opposition than measures affecting fertility. Moreover, health, dietary, and sanitation programs, those whose objective is essentially the protection of life, are initiated and executed largely by government action alone; the active support of the population at large is not really required. Consider, for example, governmental rules concerning potable water, sewage disposal, or preserving food against spoilage. The citizens whose lives depend on such government initiatives need do hardly anything at all to ensure that such policies succeed. What is required is that they should "consent" to allocate resources to such programs. And once they are even *dimly* aware of the connection between their own health and the execution of such programs, their blessing for government action in these areas is easily obtained.

How different is the case of governmental influences on birthrates? In fact, where reduction in fertility is concerned, the situation is exactly opposite. Passive consent is not sufficient; in the last analysis, success demands that each couple actively do what is required to avoid pregnancies. Reproductive behavior is regulated by powerful physiological drives and a matting of cultural values, very resistant to change, all pushing toward larger families. It takes time for governmental activity to create the conditions capable of eroding the complex and powerful structures that surround such behavior; governments must be very powerful before their intrusion into people's lives will be pervasive enough to make its impact felt on the belief and behavior of potential parents. It makes sense, therefore, to expect that decreases in death rates will precede decreases in birthrates; the length of the interval will be in large measure determined by the rate of expansion of the government's political power.

Politics and Vital Rates: Some Illustrations

The reasons we have given for the connection we allege exists between vital rates and political change are all well and good, but a cautious observer would certainly want to hear of some examples to support the hypothesis put forward here. The question at this stage is not whether we can prove or disprove this hypothesis; that is another matter, one we shall take up later in the book. The question that arises at the moment concerns, rather, what information there is suggesting that the accepted explanation of decreases in vital rates is wanting, that there are other factors at work than those allowed for in the traditional model, and that, specifically, the restructuring of the political system may turn out to be an important determinant.

There are, and there have been for some time, pieces of evidence pointing in the direction of the hypothesis presented here: even before any serious questions began to emerge regarding the demographic transition theory, there were cases that did not seem to fit what the theory said. France was most often cited as an exception. It was generally known that the French had lowered their fertility before their economic development had begun in earnest.[16] Why France did not conform to the expectations of the model nobody really seemed to know. More recently, at the beginning of the seventies, there were rumors that both birth and death rates in China were falling; but in the absence of hard evidence and in view of the history of entirely chimerical claims of this sort made since 1950 by the Chinese themselves, such rumors were not given much credence in responsible research circles until the past few years.[17] Yet, with hindsight, it seems clear that these and other cases may have offered telling indications that accepted theory had in fact overlooked one of the determinants of vital rates and that political expansion—what we call political development, previously discounted as a demographic force—was the missing link. Had we had ways of measuring the development of political systems, we might have tumbled much earlier to the relation we are exploring here.

Consider three examples from the experience of underdeveloped countries today. In all these cases, economic and social development is very *low* and unchanging, a fact that helps to control for the factors usually thought to be the main causes of change in vital rates. Moreover, the only element that "varies" from one country to another and over time is political development. If vital rates are higher in cases where political development is lower, in short, if the relation between politics and vital rates is always inverse, this will lead one to suspect that politics may indeed be a source of demographic change.

We have chosen the cases of China, Sri Lanka, and India, all countries that today fall in the category of economically underdeveloped nations. None of these nations has over the past several decades had more than two hundred or three hundred dollars per capita product per year, and all three are still very rural. There can be no doubt that, in social and economic terms, all three fall in the bottom third of the world's nations. On the other hand, each of these countries exhibits very different patterns of demographic behavior. Moreover, according to our measures, they all manifest very different levels of political effectiveness (see fig. 4). China

scores high on political effectiveness, Sri Lanka in the middle
range, and India, lowest of the three, slightly below average.[18]

In explaining the differences in demographic behavior among
these three countries, the link between political capacity and crude

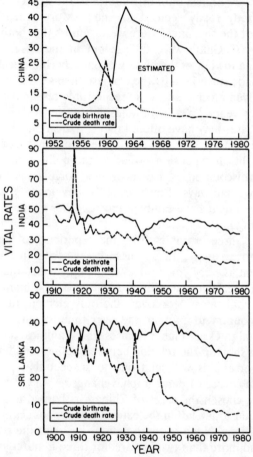

Fig. 4.   Vital rates in China, India, and Sri Lanka. Note that the vital rates
scale for India is at variance with those for China and Sri Lanka owing to an
epidemic in 1918. Note also that the time dimensions are not identical. Sources:
China—National Foreign Assessment Center, "China: A Statistical
Compendium" (July 1979), table 2, p. 5. India—India: A Statistical Outline, 4th
ed. (Calcutta, New Delhi, Bombay: Oxford and IBH Publishing Company,
1973). Sri Lanka—Department of Census and Statistics, The Population of Sri
Lanka (Colombo, 1974).

birth and death rates suggests the relationship postulated in our hypothesis. The case of India taken by itself, of course, cannot be used to support the idea that politics has any influence on vital rates; birth and death rates are high, but though the capacity of the Indian political system is low, so is socioeconomic development. But when one compares Indian demographic behavior with that of Sri Lanka and China, the pattern looked for in our hypothesis begins to emerge. Sri Lanka ranks relatively high and China very high in our estimation of the effectiveness of political systems, and their respective birth and death rates precisely match the expectations of our hypothesis.

As we shall show in detail in chapter 3, we now have rigorous measures of the capacity and effectiveness of political systems. However, even when such measures were not available, as indeed they were not until 1977, how was one to explain the way the Chinese socioeconomic system, today still almost totally rural with annual per capita income ranging between two hundred and three hundred dollars at most, has managed to reduce crude birthrates (CBR) from roughly forty-five per thousand women of childbearing age to a level of twenty-four? And if the more "incredible" Chinese claim of eighteen per thousand is true, it should be kept in mind that this rate is in the upper range of fertility levels in the developed world; some countries of the Organization for Economic Cooperation and Development (OECD), such as Spain and Greece, now have a CBR of nineteen, and Italy, Austria, Greece, and Ireland have as recently as the past decade had a CBR higher than eighteen per thousand. In the case of China, clearly, demographic behavior in line with that of developed countries cannot be associated with a modernized economy or a modernized social structure. But it can be clearly correlated with the existence of a powerful and effective political system. Political change therefore seems to offer the plausible and obvious explanation for the dramatic change in fertility.[19]

The possibility, at least, of such an interpretation has long been staring us in the face, but we have refused to see it.[20] Interestingly enough, *some* aspects of the political system were considered responsible for the decreases, one of them, not surprisingly, being family planning. Government family-planning programs are obviously a part of the operation of the political system in much the same way as a housing program or a public school system. And there seems little doubt that the Chinese effort to reduce fertility has been substantial. We assume that the birth-control program in China has had considerable effect. But, again, why was the birth-control program in China "effective" while the birth-control program in India failed to seem at least as effective? Our tentative answer is that a birth-control program will be effective only insofar as the overall effectiveness of the political system of the nation will permit.[21] In any event, we obviously believe that such effects explain only a little of the decline, by far the greatest part of the reduction in vital rates being the *unintended consequence* of the expansion and operation of the political system itself.

Some Mystifying Evidence

We should like to pursue further the question of what preliminary evidence may support our hypothesis. To this end, let us open a lengthy aside.

In the Introduction we raised the possibility that the differences between the European experience in the period before the industrial revolution and that of the developing nations of today are differences of *degree*, not of *nature*; the process at work in either case is essentially the same. But if this were in fact true, should we not find examples of European nations displaying before industrialization the same relation between politics and vital rates as that observed for India, China, and Sri Lanka? We tried to find out.

There were, of course, data problems. It should go without saying that, for the period immediately preceding the industrial revolution in Europe, we do not possess the data required for a rigorous measure of political development. To estimate political capacity, one must rely on the evaluation of social and economic historians specializing in the countries in question. To make matters worse, only a few estimates of this sort exist—for Britain, France, and Prussia. Still, however imperfect, these estimates give us something to work with. A summary of the available estimates is as follows. France is considered to have had a far more elaborate and expanded state structure than Great Britain, while Prussia is seen as having possessed the most powerful state structure of the three. The Prussian state system is, indeed, viewed as a ruthlessly efficient mechanism for raising the revenues needed to support the military machine.

The available demographic series are also estimates. Fortunately, the data match the three cases for which we also have political estimates: Britain, France, and Prussia. The results of our investigations are displayed in figure 5.[22]

The results in figure 5 are obviously the opposite of what we expected, showing a clear positive relation between levels of political development and vital rates where we hypothesized that there would be a negative relation. Prussia, judged to have had the

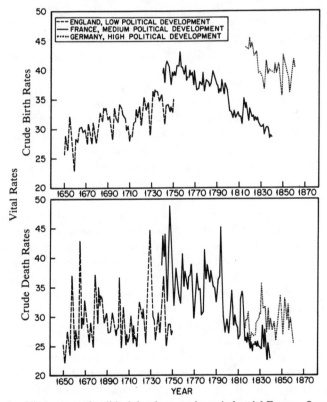

Fig. 5.   Vital rates and political development in preindustrial Europe. Sources: Germany—Gerd Hohorst, *Wirtschaftswachstrum und Bevölkerungsentwicklung in Preussen, 1816 bis 1914* (New York: Arno Press, 1977), table 11, pp. 131–32. France—Institut National d'Etudes Démographiques, "Sixième rapport sur la situation démographique de la France," *Population* 32, 2 (March–April 1977):253–338. England—E. A. Wrigley and R. S. Schofield, *The Population History of England, 1541–1871: A Reconstruction* (Cambridge: Harvard University Press, 1981), table A3.3, pp. 531–35.

most developed state system, has the highest average birthrate. France, judged to have reached a medium level of political development for the period in question, has the next highest average birthrate, though, as noted above, its vital rates decreased in the period just before the moment of economic "takeoff." And finally Britain, with the least-developed state system of the three, had the lowest average birthrate. Clearly "the data" completely contradict the hypothesis we have advanced. How is one to explain this?

There are only four possibilities: (1) The hypothesis is in some way faulty. (2) The demographic estimates are in error (we do not think this is the case). (3) The evaluations of the capacity of the state systems concerned are wrong. (4) The estimates of the relative capacity of the state structures of these three countries are roughly correct, but the progress in state building in all three cases was at the time so far below the levels required to change vital rates that other factors would be controlling birth and death rates.

Which of the four explanations should one choose?

A knee-jerk reaction would lead one to adopt the first explanation, arguing that the results are what they are because the hypothesis is wrong. We do not think so. In view of the evidence for the contemporary period, if indeed the hypothesis we advance is to be rejected, better data on the political side of the equation will be required. The second explanation leads one to the view that the data on vital rates are totally misleading. But this argument too is clearly unacceptable. Whatever one may say about the available estimates of vital rates, they are much better than the data we have on the political side.

The third way to account for the positive relation between political development and vital rates is to assume that the experts' assessments of the relative strength of the three political systems in question are wrong. This view, however, contradicts the almost universal opinion of historians. The suggestion is therefore a radical one, and we advance it only because we believe that vital rates are in fact a very good indicator of the relative capacity of political systems and that their testimony should be carefully weighed. Of course much depends on how one defines the strength or capacity of political systems. The estimates of political growth and capacity used in this book are based on government performance in collecting taxes. But in the three cases studied here, serious error could have been introduced in either (or both) of two ways: by omitting adjustments in tax bases necessary to make the performance of British, French, and Prussian governments comparable or by failing to take into account differences in methods of taxation. And regarding the latter, one can well imagine weak central elites succeeding in extracting large amounts of resources by delegating this task to private tax collectors or to local authorities.[23] Still, as long as one cannot prove that error of this sort has been committed, the best available evidence seems to bear out the accepted view of the relative strength of the three political systems involved.

We cannot yet bring ourselves to leave the matter there, however. Grant for a moment the possibility that the accepted evaluations of the relative capacity of the three governments concerned are seriously off the mark. Not only would this confirm that, as our hypothesis suggests, vital rates give an accurate indication of levels of political development, it would also entail a radical revision of our view of the relation between political and economic development.

This is an intriguing idea. Consider the implications. Current informed opinion holds that, in preindustrial Europe, strong government was inversely related to economic development.[24] In the European experience during the preindustrial era, weak government was thought to have been conducive to economic development because the stronger the state, the greater the amount of resources gobbled up by government for its own purposes, thereby reducing the pool of resources available for investment. In the developing world today, by contrast, economic development is in fact associated with strong state structures. Owing to the high cost of development in the modern, postindustrial age, strong government has come to be positively related to economic development,[25] because only a strong political system can collect the enormous amounts of resources needed for this purpose. But we shall advance the hypothesis that the apparent difference in the relation between government strength and economic development in the two epochs may be in error. May it not be possible that capable political systems have always in fact been a prerequisite of economic development and that the differences in vital rates observed in preindustrial Britain, France, and Prussia are good indicators of the relative capacity of the state structures of these countries in that preindustrial era? Such a conclusion is, of course, in line with our own view that the process of development today and in preindustrial Europe differs only in degree, not in nature.

The fourth explanation of the disparity between our findings and the predictions embedded in our hypothesis should, as we see it, be considered far more seriously. One can argue with much reason that the results one obtains for contemporary developing countries and for preindustrial Britain, France, and Prussia differ because the impact of state expansion on the life of society two hundred or three hundred years ago was only a small fraction of what it can be today. Given that communications systems in seventeenth- and eighteenth-century Europe were tenuous at best, that the vast majority of the people were villagers, and that the economy was based almost entirely on subsistence agriculture, no matter how powerful, exploitative, or oppressive a state might have been in preindustrial Europe, it would have been unlikely to make more than a faint impression on everyday life. And even this effect would have reached only a relatively small fraction of the world of villagers that made up the nation. In contrast to this, developing societies today enjoy the possibility of much more rapid political growth and massive centralization because economic, military, and communications technologies can be obtained at relatively low cost from already highly developed countries and because these support systems give the central authorities a degree of power and control quite out of keeping with the general level of development of their countries. Almost every underdeveloped country today, even those on the bottom rungs of the developmental ladder, possesses Russian, American, or Eastern or Western European tanks, planes, trucks, telephones, and hospitals. It is hardly surprising, then, that political centralization in such states is probably already more complete than in even the most powerful European state three hundred years ago. The international system makes the difference.

We argue, therefore, that the stimulus emanating from state building in preindustrial Europe was very much weaker than that observed in the developing world today. Not only was the impact of politics on vital rates in the European experience of the seventeenth and eighteenth centuries smaller in itself, but the growing political system did not enjoy, as its counterparts in today's developing world have done through much of the modern era, the explosive growth of medical, sanitary, dietary, communications, and other technologies capable of amplifying the effects of political change on demographic behavior. In sum, political activity in preindustrial Europe could not possibly have dominated the behavior of vital rates the way it can today; and as a result, the very telling effects exerted on vital rates by socioeconomic, cultural, and demographic factors inevitably succeeded in obscuring the influence of state formation.

It should be clear that this discussion of the relation between vital rates and political development in preindustrial Europe is entirely conjectural. The reader remains free, then, to dismiss it as idle speculation. Still, even as speculation, it may contribute insight into the relation between political and economic development.

Conclusion

The fundamental hypotheses underpinning the demographic transition theory appear to us correct at least in general outline. Vital rates do seem to move in response to the sort of socioeconomic and demographic change that makes up the developmental process. True, a proper specification of the causal mechanisms and a precise temporal scale are still lacking. In our view the demographic transition model can be made more useful by modifying it to allow for the influence exerted on the movement of vital rates by the massive transformations involved in political development. This is the political portion of the general developmental process. We hypothesize that change in the political system under conditions of development has a major effect on vital rates, reducing both birthrates and death rates, and that its influence on death rates will make itself felt in advance of its influence on birthrates.

This proposition could not be explored empirically in the past, for no appropriate empirical measure of "political development" existed. But it can be tested now because such a measure has at last been created. Measuring the development of political systems has proved over the past three decades a difficult and elusive problem. In the following chapter we shall describe our own attempt at devising a model that would permit the rigorous estimation of growth in the effectiveness or capacity of political systems and of the effects such growth has on vital rates.

2 The Political and Demographic Transitions

Introduction

We argued in the preceding chapter that the expansion of the political system and the consequent increase in its capacity to govern have a determining effect on vital rates. A first step on the road to testing this hypothesis is to construct a model setting forth in as much detail as may at present be possible the relation between the massive systemic transformation involved in political development and changes in rates of birth and mortality. We have furnished thus far, in our first rough sketch of socioeconomic change and vital rates, only the barest outline of what we consider this relation to be; and even less has been said about the transition from one state of political development to another.

The construction of our theoretical model consists of two steps. The first is a brief description of the massive transformation of the political system that occurs as a nation develops socially and economically. We have, of course, already given hints about what we believe this transformation comprises, and we are certain our readers will have already some conceptions of their own on this subject. But general understandings of this sort will prove insufficient. The operational components of the measure we shall propose here are rooted in a number of assumptions about the way states evolve and political systems expand. Without a comprehensive grasp of the theory underpinning what we attempt in these pages, the reader will be at a serious disadvantage in judging the value and correctness of the material we are going to present. And this first step seems all the more clearly called for inasmuch as, for students of politics, the unveiling of the new measure of political development we propose may be of greater interest than the results of the test that is the principal concern of this book. The second step in the construction of our model is an equally brief attempt to define the connection between the political transition as described in the chapter now beginning and the transition in vital rates we discussed in the chapter just brought to a close.

Let us deal, then, with the theoretical considerations relating to those elements in the expansion and centralization of central political power relevant to our problem.

Political Capacity, Political Costs, and the Extraction of Revenue

Two central components of the massive transformation the political system undergoes in the process of development are critical to our discussion: the expansion of central political power and the parallel rise in the level of taxation. The key lies in the relation between the two. Because whatever governments may wish to do will require resources, the amount of revenues they extract can be used as an indication of the level of political power attained by central authorities. The course of our analysis will be determined by the way we conceive the interaction between the accumulation of central power and taxation and the way this interaction propels the growth of the state along its path toward development. But it is not at all easy to define the process of state growth. Not only is the process of modern state building enormously complex in and of itself, but the rate and course of development may differ widely from one country to another. Then again, the patterns of "political development" today differ in many ways from the state making of preindustrial Europe. There is, moreover, no possibility of reproducing here the history of state expansion even in general outline. Fortunately, there is no need to.[1] What is required is to sketch out in a few very broad strokes the major reasons why the link between taxation and the accumulation of central political power takes the form we believe it does.

It is generally agreed that any state must perform three principal functions: maintain national security (i.e., external defense and the repression of internal rebellion or disorder), collect resources to meet collective needs, and mobilize the population for national purposes. These functions are carried out through four bureaucracies: the military forces, the national police, the civil bureaucracy, and political parties. The armed forces and national police clearly provide security and the mechanisms of internal repression; the civil bureaucracy assumes responsibility for extracting the resources the state needs; it is the task of the political parties, which function in effect as political bureaucracies, to mobilize human resources.[2]

We should warn the reader, however, that the neat distinction we have just made between the political bureaucracies mobilizing human resources and the civil bureaucracies mobilizing material resources should be regarded with a good deal of caution. Though useful for some purposes, it does not altogether correspond to the reality of what these institutions actually do, reflecting somewhat more accurately, perhaps, the reasons why these institutions were originally set up rather than the range of activities they perform once they are in place. In many systems the political parties are in fact major instruments for extracting material resources. On the other hand, the civil bureaucracy does double duty in all advanced societies, collecting material resources but also mobilizing people. For example, the delivery of the many public services supplied by modern states provides a way for governments to mobilize human resources; and military conscription is carried out almost every-where by the civil bureaucracies. In both instances the civil administration acts as the mobilizer of human resources.

The creation and development of each of these four institutions are closely related to the creation and development of the others. It is, indeed, the interrelated growth of these four bureaucracies taken together that forms the heart of the process by which, in the past, states and political systems have been built and that to this day fuels the expansion of central political power. A rough outline of the process will make this clear.

1. The process of state building begins because central elites (the state builders often referred to as the "political modernizers") require additional armed forces to protect themselves or to move against foreign and domestic enemies.

2. These new forces require additional resources to finance and supply them.

3. To collect the required resources, the state must develop a civil bureaucracy that penetrates ever more deeply into the

successive layers of the society to carry out the actual collection. During the first stage of state building this administration remains an entirely civil one. During later stages, however, when the masses begin to be integrated into a system of secondary and tertiary production, the mobilization of the nation's human resources is undertaken both by civil bureaucracies and by political parties.

4. The increase in taxation incurs resistance on the part of the population, and this requires still more resources to equip the additional armed forces needed to quell it.

5. This in turn requires a further expansion not just of the armed forces, but also of the bureaucracy, all of which creates a still greater demand for resources, in turn requiring even more taxation.

6. As the masses of the population become increasingly caught up in the economic and military machinery of the state, as productivity rises and the available pool of resources grows, the old patterns continue: more taxes are required to pay for expanding military forces and for the expanding bureaucracies responsible for extracting resources. On the other hand, new patterns are added. First a new political bureaucracy—that is, the mass political party—appears on the scene, its major function being to channel the masses entering the emerging national political system into orderly political behavior. This bureaucracy too requires resources.

Most important of all, however, government expenditures increase very rapidly. With new mass armies and increasingly advanced weapons, the costs of defense skyrocket. But increases in military spending are not the only burden. As the masses become a critical component of the system as soldiers and as labor in the new economy based on manufacturing, governments find themselves investing an ever-increasing share of available resources in the "welfare" of the population to ensure employment, old-age pensions, health, and education. Investment in welfare is not entirely eleemosynary; such expenditures are made in part to keep the population content and thus willing to work and pay taxes. After all, they can see some return on the money paid to the state. But governments also make this kind of investment because they know a healthy and educated population is more productive, and the power of the central elites depends on the population's productivity. Be that as it may, the cost of welfare and mass armies also requires additional resources. Which means more taxation, in turn requiring still more government and, again, still more resources.[3]

But, of course, the process we have described cannot last forever. There are limits to it, and these limits begin to make themselves felt as nations reach the developed level. The level of extraction cannot be so great that it takes away the resources needed to fuel the socioeconomic productive machine, enabling it to maintain if not to increase production. We are not talking here simply about the resources required to build the machines that build the machines that produce the goods that make an economy prosperous and productive. We are also talking about the resources that must be invested in human capital, primarily in the form of health care and education, to make the work force productive. This, incidentally, is one of the major sources of the constant instability of ruling coalitions in developed countries. For there is room for much debate concerning both how great a share of the available resources should be invested in human capital and also which segments of the population should benefit most thereby.

Societal needs, then, are one limit. But there is another: the political price that must be paid to impose taxation. This is an enormously important point requiring careful analysis.

But before analyzing it directly, let us look a little more closely at the pattern of political development as mirrored in extractive capacity. First, it will be obvious, in the light of what we have just said, that, given the state's almost limitless demand for revenues, charting the course of taxation is a plausible way of tracing at least in outline the development of the state and the rise of central power. As we shall see in the next chapter, the share of total product represented by taxes can indeed be used as a first step in measuring the extractive capacity of the political system; and since the government's share of national resources ought to increase as political development proceeds, extractive capacity ought to provide an accurate indication of political growth. When a nation is underdeveloped because of the poor state of its economy and the incapacity of its political system, the size of government revenue collections will be small, but the amount collected should increase as political development increases. We do not think, however, that this increase is linear. The unfolding pattern should instead look as follows. Extractive capacity should rise very slowly in the initial phase of development. One would call this the period of "primitive accumulation" of power. In a second phase, extractive capacity should rise rather steeply. This is the period of "transitional growth." A third phase occurs when the system has reached fully developed status, and growth should slow down once again. Figure 6 displays the pattern just described.

But why should this trajectory take the form of the clear S curve shown in figure 6? What forces lend that particular shape to the development of the extractive capacity of the political system and therefore to the growth of the political system itself? This is where the price governments must pay to obtain revenues comes in.

Consider. There are various political costs attached to the raising of revenues. In the first instance, very large capital investments are required to set up and maintain the mechanisms of repression, extraction, and mobilization we have just described, mechanisms essential to penetrate the society, quell resistance, and collect resources on a continuing basis to satisfy state and government needs. These costs are straightforward enough and are contained in the estimates governments prepare of the costs of maintaining military and police forces and running the bureaucracy. With skill, work, and luck, therefore, we can cull such data from government budgets. But there are other costs that are a little harder to estimate. These are the additional political costs that central authorities must pay to win over powerful groups of

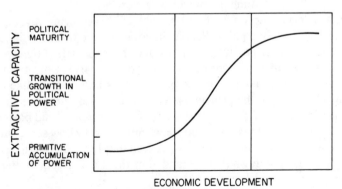

Fig. 6. Economic development and extractive capacity.

elites that, supported by segments of the mass of the population, resist contributing to state revenues and make extraction of such resources difficult if not impossible.

In this regard we should begin by noting that when political leaders—finance ministers, prime ministers, heads of state—decide whether to tax for certain purposes and how much of a contribution to demand, they enjoy a great deal less freedom than one would normally suppose. One should keep in mind that the power of political leaders to rule is everywhere delegated to them as representatives of a coalition comprising most if not all of the factions and special interests that effectively *wield power* in a given society. Participation in a coalition means protection for the producers of resources, who wish to defend as much as possible of their wealth for their own use against the demands made by governing elites (or other elites) that they be used on behalf of the collectivity as a whole or for special groups within that collectivity. Nonparticipation or weak representation in the ruling coalition should almost inevitably mean either bearing a proportionately higher burden of taxation or enjoying decreased access to collective resources. No more difficult or more politically explosive decision has to be made by any ruling coalition than that concerning who shall contribute how much and for what. Increasing the burden of taxation inevitably raises questions of who gives and who receives, and the struggle for political power is essentially a struggle over decisions of this kind. Nothing can be more divisive, and politically at least the costs may be exorbitant and impossible to meet. Errors of judgment here may unglue the coalition and threaten the government's power to govern.

Considering the political costs involved in acquiring revenues leads us to a second point. People do not like to be taxed, and they resist it whenever possible.[4] The history of the growth of the state is punctuated by rebellions against taxation in all its various forms. The distaste for taxation on the part of elites and masses alike is, ironically enough, the principal reason why taxation provides such a good indicator of governmental development, reach, and power. For the amount of tax collected shows quite clearly how successful the government is in making its people comply with government policy even though what is demanded of them may not be in their immediate interest.[5]

The problem of compliance in the field of taxation is an

immensely complicated subject. Why people pay taxes or why they tend to evade them is influenced by cultural, psychological, and other factors. Until recently, Americans complied willingly with the demands of their government. Rumor has it that this pattern is now changing. The French and the Italians, on the other hand, are notorious for having made tax evasion as great an art as some of their painting and literature. Why such differences should exist across cultures is difficult to say. Be that as it may, large-scale noncompliance, whatever its origin, signals a diminution in governmental control. Thus the appearance of substantial black market economies, for example, is an important and unmistakable sign of a decline in a given government's potency.

Resistance to central authority is not always the same, however; its nature changes as development proceeds. We shall touch upon two points in this connection. The first concerns the varying intensity of resistance as political development passes from one stage to another, and the second relates to the role of political parties. Regarding the first, it should be noted that, at the beginning of the expansion of central authority, resistance to penetration and to the extraction of resources is very strong. Local groups, held together by ties of religion or language or a history of autonomy or sometimes all three at once, fight desperately to keep free of central rule and escape incorporation into the larger national unit. This resistance, led by local elites, is usually overcome in favor of the central authority by force of arms over a period of several generations. Read the story of Sweden or Russia, of Italy, France, or Germany in the seventeenth, eighteenth, and nineteenth centuries, or the story of Pakistan, India, Indonesia, Iran, Iraq, or so many of the countries of Africa today—it is everywhere a tale of local wars, of alliances among local lords against the central authority, of the constant maneuvering of the central authority to divide and conquer its enemies. This struggle lies at the heart of all histories dealing with the creation of states.

But it should be noted that, by and large, midway along the developmental trajectory the military forces, the police, and the bureaucratic bodies that constitute the repressive and extractive mechanisms of the state are already solidly in place. Rebellion at the periphery has been crushed; the state has "won" its internal battle, at least for the time being. One would hypothesize that this is the point at which the power of the central political elite has reached its maximum. The sources of former resistance have been eliminated, and new opposition has yet to emerge. In such situations, political power and political flexibility are at their apogee.

As development continues, however, new groups begin to take shape, destined to become, often decades later, the sources of effective resistance to central authority in general and to governmental extraction of resources in particular. The difference between the resistance offered by such collectivities at the beginning and in the second half of the developmental trajectory is that the latter resistance is largely, albeit by no means entirely, nonviolent, has far more power behind it, and, most important, proves far more effective than the former.

The resistance offered to the central elite in the very last phase of the developmental process is rooted in two major politico-economic consequences of the industrial revolution. As development unfolds, the new socioeconomic structure gives rise to an enormous number of coalitions of both producers and consumers seeking political help and redress either to diminish their own tax burden or to obtain additional benefits for themselves out of common funds. The economic leaders owe their power to their possessing the means of production and to their control over the capital required to finance economic growth. This usually earns them admission to the ruling coalition; and, indeed, the leaders of the new economy gain access to political power very early on.[6] The masses, on the other hand, derive their influence over political decisions from their incorporation in the new productive machine as workers and consumers, their chief source of power being the services they render as a labor force. But the masses not only man the economic system; they also provide the sinew for the rapidly expanding military apparatus. Since work and fighting are the twin pillars on which the power of the state and its leaders rests, the authorities have in the end little option but to accede at least in part to the wishes of the people.

These collectivities, whose leaders are for the most part themselves members of the ruling coalition or at least have partial or indirect access to it, soon have their views well represented by members of the government prepared to defend their interests against other government leaders; and all this, of course, makes

obtaining cooperation and resources from them even more difficult. These groups use every political avenue they can to put
pressure on the central authorities. All political institutions—the
judiciary, the legislature, the bureaucracies—become the arenas
in which the struggle over resources and power is waged, and the
process through which this struggle is carried out is enormously
complex. The ferocious and effective resistance the different
factions put up to government demands for their resources or to
government actions perceived to be contrary to their interests, and
the maneuverings of the government seeking to head off or quell
this resistance, form the basic stuff of the story of the current
politics of every developed country in the world no matter how
powerful or hegemonic the ruling political elite may appear to be.

Which brings us to the second of the two points mentioned
above. In developing and developed countries alike, political
parties provide one of the main political arenas in which special
interest groups fight to defend their interests. The role of parties in
democratic politics is well known. In democratic systems, the
political parties are a recognized channel for influences running
from the bottom up. Through them, segments of the masses and
nonpolitical elites set limits on the government elites running the
state apparatus, and the party also serves as a training ground
where its members acquire the skills to influence those at the
controls of the machinery of the state. But we also alluded earlier
to the role the party plays in channeling powerful currents flowing
the other way, from the top down. Indeed, parties are primarily
institutions through which political elites mobilize the masses,
channel their behavior into orderly procedures, engineer acceptance of the legitimacy of their own rule, and manipulate public
opinion to gain consent for the costs of achieving national goals.

Clearly, then, as an institution the party does double duty,
allowing leaders to mobilize the masses and in turn enabling the
masses to impose limits on central government elites. Which of
these two roles proves dominant in any given case depends on a
great many factors, but there is one particularly important distinction.

The motive power for the expansion of political parties from
relatively small associations into giant institutions accommodating
mass memberships originates in elites' efforts to prevail over other

elites or over external enemies. The character and activity of a given political party are likely to differ markedly depending on the conditions under which it becomes a mass party. For the party may expand into a mass institution *as a result* of economic development or it may do so *before* economic development has taken place, itself serving as a major instrument in engendering economic growth. The part it ultimately plays in this connection will define its essential nature and function. If the development of the political party follows on economic development (the experience in Western Europe and European countries overseas), "the party" will tend to function much less as an effective tool for mobilizing mass adherence to government policies than as a medium for representing the section that opposes government leaders. In other words, when the rise of the party comes about as a by-product of economic growth, the party itself becomes a channel for resistance to the wishes of the state on the part of the economic elites and popular forces that emerge as a result of socioeconomic development. On the other hand, if the growth of the party precedes economic development and the party serves as a major instrument in fostering such development, then its role is far more likely to be that of an instrument of control over people's behavior, acting as a handmaiden to the civil bureaucracy in extracting resources and seconding the mechanism of repression in the state.

Some illustrations will help us make the point. In modern Western democracies, for example, where economic growth has in the main antedated political development, the party is often far more a channel of resistance than a tool of mobilization. By contrast, in the communist countries of Europe, where profound development had to await the extensive socioeconomic reorganization effected by the Communist party, the party is primarily (though not exclusively) an instrument of state direction, control, and repression. This is far more true of the communist systems of East and Southeast Asia, where all resistance to central authority on the part of autonomous local communities has been destroyed, where socioeconomic growth has still not really begun, and where the power of economic and other interest groups ranges from very weak to nonexistent.

Let us return to the main point. The developmental process

engenders resistance. We are not used to thinking of central authorities as provoking the resistance they meet, yet it is clear that they are at least a major, if not the major, offender in this regard. When armed internecine conflict breaks out, the forces of the state may not strike the first blow, but expanding government power and the accompanying demand for resources are the underlying cause of the conflict.[7]

Thus far in this discussion, we have separated the various types of resistance into two neat categories. We have made it appear as if violent resistance to early state expansion and the ever greater violence with which the state crushes this resistance were entirely a feature of the preindustrial era. We have also made it appear as if the dogged, but legal and nonviolent resistance to the demands of the state in the form of lobbying, parliamentary opposition, and civil disobedience were to be found solely after economic systems reach a high level of development. But this, of course, is not the case. One finds a good deal of foot dragging and successful manipulation of central power by groups within society even before the hegemony of the central authority has been established; and violent resistance to central authority reemerges frequently even after nations have reached fully developed status. Unfortunately, development does not necessarily mean peace. Think of the separatists, the terrorists, the leaders of revolutionary movements in Spain, Greece, Cyprus, Italy, Germany, and Northern Ireland. Virtually no developed country is entirely immune to outbreaks of violence. But the *kind* of resistance opposed to central political authority is not at issue here so much as the *cost*; and it is the *costs* of containing such resistance that indicate the level of capacity governments have achieved. It should be firmly borne in mind, of course, that political capacity is seen in relation to the economic resources available, the state's ability to govern being reflected in the percentage of total product it succeeds in directing to its own purposes.

The relation between economic development and extractive capacity as indicated by the political costs of tax collection should be very different from the pattern established between the share of total product collected by the government and economic growth. Political capacity should be low, and political costs should be very high at the beginning of development. Political costs should go down steeply thereafter up through the first half of the developmental trajectory, and this drop should be accompanied by a sharp rise in extractive capacity. But costs should rise steeply again once the nation achieves developed status, and the extractive capacity of the political system should stabilize. Figure 7 suggests the relation one would expect to find between the costs of political extraction, the extractive capacity of the system, and economic development.

It is clear that the two curves do not move in parallel fashion at all, yet the movement of the one can be used as an indicator of the movement of the other. The reason is to be found in the explanation we have just given concerning how and why political costs affect the extractive capacity of the system in the precise way they do.

Our account of the reasons for and consequences of the expansion of states' efforts to collect resources from their people raises exactly the same methodological problem that faced the authors of the demographic transition theory some fifty years ago (see chap. 1). To grasp the nature of the process we are concerned with here, we have to chart the full trajectory of the development of the political system from the initial stage when the centralization of power has not yet begun, and therefore the nucleus of state-building elites is at best only primus inter pares among the rival power groups in the country, to the stage of power maturity when, regardless of government forms, power has effectively been

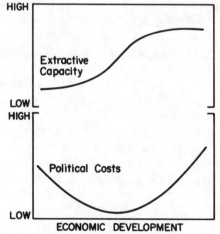

Fig. 7. Economic development, political costs, and extractive capacity.

centralized. But this requires a series of data stretching back two centuries or more. Because the necessary data simply do not exist, we are obliged to fall back on exactly the same method adopted in elaborating the theory of the demographic transition. Our design, in other words, will involve taking a cross section of the present international system, which includes underdeveloped, developing, and developed nations, and assuming that the interaction between taxation and political power in each of these three groups will represent the fundamental features of the corresponding stage of the historical dynamic described in this chapter.

As we pointed out earlier regarding the use of this method in constructing the demographic transition theory, the assumption that the developing world of today will follow in the footsteps of contemporary developed nations is dubious. We still believe this assumption is valid, however. True, the processes of development vary widely across countries and over time owing to marked differences in technology and population pressures and owing to fluctuations in start-up costs since currently developed nations set out on the road to development. Yet the underlying dynamic of development changes very little, at least in its essentials. What does vary is the catalytic influence that changes in any one sector of national life exert on other sectors. But, again, we cannot claim to have proved that a cross-sectional view of the current system can be regarded as an accurate representation of the dynamic of politicoeconomic development as it has unfolded in the historical experience of today's developed countries.[8] Nor, a fortiori, can we claim that it provides a genuine insight into the nature of politico-economic development. We simply assume this is the case while admitting that there is at present no way to validate this assumption empirically. For the moment, the true value of this method remains a matter for theoretical debate.

Here an important point needs to be made. It is clear that, in the contemporary era, state building and the expansion of the political system can proceed a very long way without concurrent socioeconomic development. This trend is particularly visible in the case of communist nations of East Asia such as Vietnam, China, and North Korea. The achievements of these nations in building up their political systems to the extent that they have suggests that the process of state building under today's conditions is *far* more independent of concurrent socioeconomic change than was true in the European experience at the same point in the trajectory of development. But this greater degree of independence from socioeconomic development is precisely what highlights the influence of political development on vital rates.

Another point demanding attention is that the measure of political costs we have devised (see chaps. 3 and 4) seeks to separate the impact of political growth from that of economic growth. However, it succeeds in doing so only imperfectly. As will be seen below, we dealt with this problem at the operational level by controlling for gross national product in our analysis.

And yet another matter requires some comment here. Our belief that differences exist in the severity of the political costs different countries pay in extracting resources from their societies is also almost entirely inferential, based on the way we think the process of state building works. Our inference provides an answer to a fascinating question. Why are the political systems of some countries so much more effective than those of others at a similar level of socioeconomic development? Is it correct, as so many observers are wont to say, that the difference lies in their willingness to make the necessary effort? This view has a certain surface plausibility, but when one thinks of concrete cases one is troubled. Why, throughout all the years of its struggle with the North, did South Vietnam fail to attain the same level of political effectiveness as the North? It had every reason and every opportunity to do so. It seems plausible to argue that the South tried, but failed, and paid with its life as a result. The same question arises with respect to many other countries. Why has not India's political system, for instance, managed to become as effective as China's? The Indians seem able only to talk a good game: Why so little action? Nor are South Vietnam and India alone in this. No matter how great and visible their need, no matter how hard they try, many countries do not seem able to develop politically. What makes it so difficult for them to scale the rungs of the developmental ladder? It is not, in our view, simply for lack of trying. What, then, holds them back?

We think the key to an explanation is that the laggards must pay increasingly large costs *at the margin* in order to extract additional resources; and given the social, economic, and political structures of their countries, they simply do not have the wherewithal to meet this need. The costs central governments must pay at the margin to acquire fresh resources vary profoundly and predictably for countries traveling along the developmental continuum. The matter is not fundamentally dissimilar to the predicament in which any private person may find him or herself when seeking to borrow money. The interest charged sets limits on how much, if any, of the necessary money can be borrowed. The marginal costs of extracting resources represent, then, the interest that must be paid if nations are to improve their political performance. Our theory leads us to expect that these marginal costs are high at the underdeveloped and developed levels, but that they are low for developing countries, that is, at the intermediate stage in the process of development. We shall return to this point below.

Political Power and Vital Rates

Everything we have had to say about the growth of the state, about the way the growth of the state is related to the growth of the extractive capacity of the political system, and about the way both are related to the evolution of political costs is critical in defining the model of the link between politics and rates of births and deaths proposed in this book. The important question is, of course, how the interaction between economic and political growth and the costs associated with extracting resources is related to the movement of vital rates described in the preceding chapter. We shall try very briefly to show how all these factors come together, thus adding the final piece to the model of the connection between politics and demography. We shall then be ready to undertake the empirical analyses detailed in the chapters that follow.

Establishing the link between the political transition as defined in this chapter and the demographic transition as described in the last chapter is an intricate task. Its complexity stems from the fact that we must bring political capacity, political costs, vital rates, and economic development into relation to each other, even though each of these variables evolves along quite different lines of its own. Bringing together the movements posited for each of the variables bearing on the demographic and political transitions, we obtain the model depicted in figure 8. Note that extractive capacity is represented simply by taxation adjusted for policy preferences.

We have hard data at our disposal for this variable, as also for vital rates. For political costs, on the other hand, as we shall see in the next chapter, we have had to use an estimate.

The model displayed in figure 8 suggests that there are both positive and negative relations between vital rates and political behavior. If we look at vital rates and extractive capacity we see that, as capacity goes up, vital rates come down. Very roughly, then, the relation is inverse. On the other hand, when we look at the relation between vital rates and political costs the picture is somewhat confused. In phases 1 and 2, corresponding roughly to the stages reached by the underdeveloped and developing nations of the world, the relation is distinctly positive: as political costs go down, so do vital rates. But at the developed level things at first seem quite messy. As nations begin the climb from developing to developed status costs go up, but the descending curve of fertility and mortality flattens out. There seems, then, to be no relation

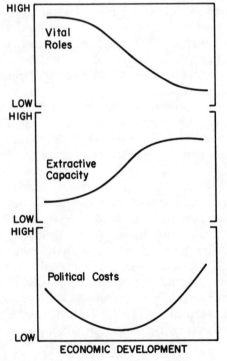

Fig. 8. The political and demographic transition model.

between births and deaths on the one hand and the political costs of extracting resources on the other.

How is one to explain this apparent lack of connection? First of all, we assume that a connection does in fact exist. The reasons why vital rates and the costs of extraction nevertheless seem unconnected are, we believe, as follows. As we indicated when we discussed the link between political costs and extractive capacity, the extractive capacity of the system decreases and flattens out as costs increase. But, of course, the other side of the equation is also affected. When the share of the total product extracted by government stops increasing, the costs no longer continue to rise; they stabilize as well. In the second place, it seems entirely reasonable to argue that there will be a lag between the halt in the rise in costs and the cessation of the rise in the curve of extractive capacity; for it is at that point where the costs become "too high" that growth in the rate of extraction subsides. A similar lag will, moreover, be observed in the relation between extractive capacity and vital rates. As costs continue to rise, though more slowly, and extractive capacity ceases to increase, politics ceases to push vital rates downward. And as a result of the consequent stabilization of pressures from the economic and social sides, vital rates also eventually stabilize.

This, then, is our theoretical model of the link between vital rates and politics, setting forth our expectations of how political and demographic behavior will evolve in relation to each other and the reasons why the relation between the two should take this form. Now that we have armed ourselves with a model of how political and demographic variables interact, thus enabling us to give our theory testable form, let us turn to the problems of rendering our constructs operational.

3 The Operationalization of the Measures

Introduction

We have pointed out that the reason the effects of political development on fertility and mortality have not been tested before lies in the absence of a rigorous measure of the independent variable, political development. Now that such a measure has been constructed, however, such an analysis at last becomes possible. This enables us, moreover, to test our hypothesis that growth in political capacity and change in vital rates are inversely related—that increase in the capacity to govern will be reflected in a decline in rates of births and deaths. Our next step is to give a detailed account of exactly how we arrived at the index of political development we are going to use here. The measure in question is, after all, entirely new and not yet in common use, so a detailed account of what went into its elaboration and how it has been used will be of particular interest.[1]

Let us recall some of the points made in the preceding chapter. In our view the extraction of resources is a critical measure of the government's capacity to meet the wider demands placed upon it by its own elites, and also by the masses of the population and the foreign and domestic socioeconomic environments in which all political systems are lodged. Taxes give an excellent indication of governmental presence and penetration, for there is no other operation of government so heavily dependent on mass support and the government's ability to instill respect and even fear in the population. Rarely, moreover, are individuals so directly and massively affected by government; even more rarely, whether as individuals or as collectivities, do they so vigorously resist government intrusion into their private lives. And yet without some form of taxation there can be no national purpose, and success or failure in imposing taxes and extracting revenue therefore supplies a perfect indicator of a government's capacity to obtain and maintain real popular support.[2] Thus it is natural to use taxes and other forms of revenue data to construct our measures.

Let us turn, then, to the operationalization of our measure of political development.

The Political Measure and Its Components

We shall do two things. First, we shall describe in very general terms how the measure has been constructed. Then we shall pass on to a detailed description of the way the components of the measure have been rendered operational, how they fit together, and why the construction of our index took the form it did.

In our index the measurement of the political costs incurred by governments in raising taxes, a matter discussed at some length in the previous chapter, is used as an indicator of the political system's capacity to perform its various functions. In its bare bones, the measure being proposed is as follows.

We estimate "the maximum" that a given political system could possibly extract, then subtract from this "maximum value" what the system has "actually extracted." We next adjust both values to ensure that economic differences do not confound the evaluation of political performance. Finally, we take the difference between the two adjusted values to represent the share the government has not been able to extract. Assuming that governments extract all they can, this share expresses the magnitude of political costs— the higher the costs, the smaller the share relative to the maximum.

The reader may find this roundabout way of measuring political capacity rather amusing. Tortuous though it may be, however, this procedure is the only one available so long as it remains impossible to measure directly all the components of political costs of extraction. This inferential measurement procedure, bizarre though it may seem, is not without parallel in the natural sciences. One is reminded of Max Delbruck's[3] charming comment concerning the study of bacteriophage viruses before the electron microscope had been introduced:

> One might wonder how the biologist can learn anything about the behavior of organisms so small. . . . The answer is that the bacterial viruses make themselves known by the bacteria they destroy, as a small boy announces his presence when a piece of cake disappears.

Governments, of course, are not little boys, but they too, perhaps, make their strength known by the slice of the revenue pie they wanted but were unable to get. And if this is the case, then the *size* of the slice, once it is known how big it might have been under ideal conditions, should give us a fair idea of their capacity and strength.

The measure we propose, then, contains three major components:

a.   The first is the estimation of the maximum amount a state could possibly be expected to extract if it had the necessary tools and set about extracting resources from its people with all its might.

b.   The second component is the share of the total product the state has actually collected, that is, the state's actual extractive capacity.

c.   The third is the measure of the political costs of extraction, which determine the point at which the state has to stop extracting resources on its way to the maximum.

A further element enters the picture, however, one that is not a component of the model as such but an inference based on of the results we obtain. This additional element is the conception of the *marginal* political costs paid by the state in levying resources. We shall have occasion to return to this element, already discussed in the preceding chapter, during our account of how our model works.

Let us now turn to a closer definition of each of these three major components of the measure, to the discussion of the reasoning behind them, and to the more detailed explanation of the indicators used in each case.

The Actual Extractive Capacity of the System

Let us begin with the extractive capacity of the system. As the reader is by now aware, we shall use taxation—taxes actually collected—as our measure of extractive capacity. Extractive capacity is used as an indicator of the *overall* capacity of the system, by which we mean its capacity to perform the tasks imposed on it by the domestic and foreign environments in which any political system is rooted. It is not possible at present to assess directly the growth and performance of various political institutions that make for political capacity. To do this one would first need to analyze the formation of the political coalitions required to make decisions, the operational codes employed in such decision making, and the performance of the political networks linking elites and masses together so as to permit the former to mobilize and draw on the support of the latter. Then one would need to determine the contribution each of these factors makes to the capacity of the system as a whole, combining the values derived for the different components to come up with a total. Were it possible to do all these things, our problems would be solved. The fact remains that it is not. Nevertheless, for the reasons discussed earlier, the ability to extract resources is a good indication of the overall capacity of the political system; and the use of revenue data is certainly a first step in measuring differences in the extractive capacity of the various countries in the international system.

We should note, however, that the share of resources obtained by a government has major limitations as a comparative measure of the capacity of governments unless one also has a standard against which the performance of each government can be evaluated. The maximum is used as such a standard.

Moreover, although theoretically taxes are almost an ideal indicator of the extractive capacity of the system, taxation or revenue levels cannot be used directly as an indicator of the political component of extractive capacity. The taxes actually collected in any country are always the product of the operation of both the economic and the political subsystems of the national society. One cannot be sure, then, on the basis of total revenue alone, what part of the total is to be imputed to the contribution made by each of the subsystems on its own, and one cannot therefore estimate directly the performance of the political system per se. Taxes, then, furnish our measure of the extractive capacity of the political system, but this measure unfortunately confounds economic and political factors; nor have we a direct means of disentangling the two. Even the use of a tax ratio does not sufficiently eliminate the presence of economic factors. But if we cannot directly distinguish between the respective contributions of the political and economic subsystems, we have managed to do so indirectly. Introducing the conception of maximum extractable revenues and using political costs as the ultimate measure of political capacity, as discussed below, offers a better way of distinguishing economic from political effects. We should make it clear that we can never distinguish completely between economic and political effects. Whatever indexes we may develop for this purpose must therefore remain fairly crude and approximate.

Another point needs to be raised. We should note, first of all, that any model must assume that the system's performance is equivalent to its capacity—that capacity, in other words, can be inferred directly from performance. But in constructing a model one must also take pains to minimize the suspicion that the level of extraction of resources reflects not only systemic capacity but also personal capacities and preferences of political leaders as individuals; that is, that a country's performance in raising taxes is in part a function of the character and will of individual political leaders, inevitably implying that a good deal of the variation in tax performance from one country to another arises because some political leaders are able and willing to put their shoulders to the wheel and push while others are not. This interpretation, though perfectly plausible and the intuitive reaction of many observers to events on the political scene, is fundamentally flawed. Moreover, were this viewpoint adopted without qualification, it would cast serious doubt on any attempt to measure political capacity by measuring the collection of revenues. For if it is possible for leaders to extract less than their system will yield simply because they fail or refuse to try hard enough, how is one to know whether poor performance in this regard represents the system's inability to raise the necessary resources or merely leaders' personal inability or unwillingness to extract them?

Our own interpretation of the problem is that levels of taxation are in very large measure "decided" by political structures; that is, by the political coalitions formed by elites and their clientele that make up the power structures of any country. They are not therefore imputable to the will of a finance minister or even a head of state.[4] We argue, in other words, that some governments perform better in extracting resources than others not because their political leaders have more backbone, but because the political coalitions that thrust such leaders into positions of power permit them to impose that much more taxation. This may seem a difficult view to accept, but the reader should be aware that the model we present here contains such an assumption. We, of course, believe it is valid. We recognize, however, that there is as yet no way to demonstrate its truth by empirical means, and the reader may feel more comfortable in granting it solely as a working hypothesis, suspending judgment for the moment as to its accuracy. We shall return to this problem in our discussion of political costs.

Maximum Extractive Capacity

Let us now move on to the second component of our model and the problem of determining the maximum extractive capacity to which political systems can aspire.

As we have already indicated, in making the subtraction that will yield the index of actual political capacity at the heart of our model, the subtrahend is provided by the total of the taxes the state manages to collect. To be sure, as we shall see more particularly below, some adjustments will have to be made to this figure, but establishing the subtrahend will prove straightforward enough. But what is the minuend?

The second key to the operation of our model rests on establishing the absolute upper limit on what governments can extract from their societies. Conceptually, establishing the maximum possible share of total available resources a government may hope to obtain is simple. We may define this maximum by taking the case of that nation in which the government, endowed with the necessary political tools and single-minded commitment, has demonstrated more than any other the ability either to persuade or to compel the population under its authority to surrender into its hands the resources it needs. The performance of this government may then serve as a standard by which to assess the performance of other governments. But if defining what we mean by "maximum

extractive capacity" presents no special difficulties in principle, the
practical problem remains of determining how one is to render this
concept operational. How do we actually establish what this
maximum is? How do we choose which country should serve as a
standard for comparison?

The problem is intriguing, and the way we propose to solve
it—the method we shall follow in seeking to identify the country
that will best serve as a standard of comparison—is to observe the
tax performance of countries engaged in *total war*. For it makes
sense to think that the governments of nations locked in mortal
combat, where the liberty and even the existence of each comba-
tant will depend on the outcome of the fighting, will try their
hardest, and that both masses and elites, faced with the grim
reality of what the loss of the war would mean, would be ready to
make the maximum sacrifice required of them.

Fortunately we dispose of the results of previous research in
which, in an attempt to find a means of predicting the outcomes of
international conflicts, experiments have been carried out with
measures of political and national capabilities. The best performance posted by any of the combatants in the wars examined in this
research will became the standard used here.

Among the combatants in the conflicts studied[5] (and one should
repeat that in these conflicts all the principal combatants fought
with all their might for their very lives, thus assuring us of the
wholeheartedness of their efforts, the maximum possible extraction of resources being literally a matter of life or death) there
were two nations, one from the ranks of developing countries and
one from the already developed world, that extracted far more
resources than any other nation in any war for which data were
available. The nations in question were North Vietnam during the
recent conflict between that nation and South Vietnam (helped by
the United States) and Great Britain in World War II. North
Vietnam extracted 47 percent of its gross national product from its
population during the Vietnam War, and Britain, in its fight
against Hitler, allocated 54 percent of its gross product to defense.
The two proportions do not represent exactly the same thing, of
course, since in the case of the British the fraction of the total
product indicates only what was specifically allocated to the war
effort. They are nevertheless similar enough to be used together
without problem.[6] We did feel, however, that the estimates for

North Vietnam might be too extreme to serve as a reasonable standard for all other developing countries, and we knew that the fraction expended by the Vietnamese for defense would be smaller than the total share Britain extracted from the GNP for this purpose. To be as conservative as possible, therefore, the maximum share one would expect could conceivably be extracted by a government and devoted to a single, specified purpose was adjusted to 40 percent for developing countries and to 55 percent for developed countries: 40 percent and 55 percent then became the maximums used for nondeveloped and developed nations respectively.

No other country ever achieved the levels of extraction realized by North Vietnam and Great Britain. It seems reasonable to argue, then, that British and Vietnamese performance in the hour of greatest national danger could be taken as a fair indication of the maximum level of extraction possible by developed and developing countries. Thus, if all other developing countries had the political system possessed by North Vietnam and found themselves under the same necessity, they too would be able to extract for a single purpose the same proportion of resources. Similarly, all developed nations would be able to match British performance in World War II if only they had Britain's political capacity.

Here, an aside. If the extraction of resources provides an excellent indicator of the general capacity of a political system, and if the levels of extraction attained by Britain and North Vietnam in fact furnish a rough but generally accurate indication of the maximum political capacity of developed and developing countries, then we catch in this *glimpse* of a possible solution to a problem that has never been approached before: an insight into the size of the contribution socioeconomic development can make to political development. How much more can a political system extract once the national society has achieved a high level of economic development? The maximums we have chosen for North Vietnam and Great Britain give us some indication, for the size of the contribution made by economic to political development should be very roughly equal to the difference between the maximums established for developing and developed countries. In other words, the magnitude of the increase achieved in political development through social and economic development will be on the order of 10 to 15 percent more in extractive capacity. But that is so only if one assumes that North Vietnam and Great Britain were political "equals" in extracting resources from their populations.

A second point. Our findings suggest that there is no relation between the form of government and the capacity to govern. Great Britain was a democracy while its major antagonist was a totalitarian dictatorship, yet Britain bested Hitler's Germany by a substantial margin. North Vietnam, on the other hand, was a totalitarian dictatorship, yet its performance in raising resources while being bombed and blockaded, and with its youth decimated by the war, was incredible. It should be kept in mind, moreover, that North Vietnam had a per capita product of only slightly more than one hundred dollars per year. One certainly could not argue, therefore, that the government of Ho Chi Minh succeeded in extracting so high a level of resources because the Vietnamese people had riches to spare for their government. The implications of this matter, if confirmed by later research, will prove of the utmost significance for the study of politics.[7]

Adjustments of Actual and Maximum Taxation Levels

The two critical elements in our model are the maximum potential level of extraction and the amount of revenue actually taken in by governments in the form of taxes. But the two values obtained in this connection require adjustment.

The need to impose controls is easy to explain. Given our desire to employ the extraction of resources as an indicator of relative government performance, it is essential that one correct for features in the national systems that, left untouched, may seriously distort our results when comparisons are made.

Two sets of differences are particularly relevant. The first concerns the policy preferences of the elites and their publics. After all, when we attempt to evaluate political capacity and performance we must take into account just what it is that governments are trying to do. The government of Sweden, for example, prefers to take care of the health needs of Swedes through the public sector and therefore must tax the Swedish people to defray the costs of these health services. The United States government, on the other hand, provides for health needs through the private sector. It does not, consequently, tax the American people for a service it does not perform, with the result that the overall level of taxation is lower in the United States than in Sweden. It would be foolish, however, to think of the United States government as less capable of fulfilling its basic responsibilities than the Swedish political system simply because American tax levels are lower than those of Sweden. Some sort of adjustment will, then, have to be made to correct for the policy preferences reflected in the respective levels of taxation of these two countries.

The other factor one must adjust for consists of differences in the tax bases of the various countries in the international system. When we consider the maximum possible share that governments can be expected to extract from the pool of total national resources, it becomes clear that some countries enjoy a pronounced economic advantage over others. Specifically, large numbers of countries in the contemporary international system have large mineral deposits or are considerable producers of agricultural commodities sold on the world market, and this agricultural or mineral wealth places substantial sources of revenues at the disposal of their governments. Some nations, then, have very prosperous economies while others rely almost entirely on subsistence agriculture: Some countries dispose of vast mineral resources or are major exporters of highly prized commodities that yield them a favorable balance of international trade, while others are forced to import large quantities of goods. The task of government in collecting taxes thus becomes far easier or far more difficult depending on the economic circumstances, and if these circumstances are not properly taken into account our evaluation of government performance could be seriously distorted. In the case of the Organization of Petroleum Exporting Countries (OPEC), for example, given the colossal revenues derived from oil, it would clearly be a mistake to conclude solely on the basis of unadjusted data relating to taxation that the governments of these countries are more capable than the governments of other, less fortunate nations. And, indeed, if one controls for the enormous share of their revenues represented by oil income, the governments of the OPEC nations drop in any measure of capacity toward the bottom of the pile, where they belong. Thus the need to control for advantages or disadvantages in the tax bases of the countries should be plain.

The data we used relating to taxes were, then, adjusted to reflect policy preferences, and the maximum level of extraction was adjusted to allow for variations in the size of the tax base. Regarding the latter set of adjustments, we tried a number of controls. Some were retained, but others, failing to make adequate allowance for advantages or disadvantages in the tax base, were discarded. It should be noted, moreover, that the adjustments effected here should be considered nothing more than what, in the parlance of the trade, is called "a first cut." Experiments are needed to elaborate more refined controls than those used here.

Yet another point needs to be made in this connection. The adjustments in our estimate of the maximum share of resources that governments can be expected to extract and in the levels of taxation that they actually achieve were different in the case of developing countries from those we made for developed nations.

Let us begin by describing the adjustments we made to control for differences in policy preferences in the taxes of developing and developed countries. First, we excluded nontax revenues. Second, given the appalling needs and the enormous lack of resources experienced in the developing world, governments do not have much choice in the expenditures they make; very few services can be provided at a very low economic level. Social security is the only major area in the realm of expenditures in which differences are found. Some countries spend a significant proportion of the little they have on social security while others do not. It should be noted that, in the case of taxes collected for social security, governments exercise no discretion; they simply gather funds earmarked for a specific purpose and immediately redistribute them. But discretionary funds are precisely the ones we are interested in as an indicator of political capacity. The adjustment made to correct for social security payments was therefore quite simple: we subtracted social security taxes from the total taxes collected.

Adjusted extraction ratio = (general government revenue − nontax revenue − social security contributions)/GDP

In the case of developed countries, however, more is required to assess not only what governments take from the population, but also what they give back. In addition to adjusting for social security benefits, we had to apply two further controls in estimating the taxes collected in these nations. One control was for health expenditures and the other was for expenditures in education: expenditures that, alongside social security benefits, represent between them the major source of government spending for the welfare of their populations. There is a good deal of variation from one developed country to another in the level of expenditures for health and education.

However, such differences are effectively eliminated by introducing social security expenditures into the model. Thus the adjusted extraction ratio for developed countries is estimated as follows:

Adjusted extraction ratio = (general government revenue − nontax revenue − social security expenditures)/GDP

Let us now turn to a brief account of the way we adjusted the estimates of the maximum possible share of total national resources that governments could be expected to collect in the form of taxes in developing and developed countries. As we indicated earlier, our concern centered on possible distortions stemming from the fact that some countries possess great mineral wealth or large export sectors in their economies while others do not, a circumstance that risks severely biasing comparisons of government performance in taxation. Such economic assets make it considerably easier to raise revenues, in part because it is simple for governments to tax exports or the mining of minerals and in part because of the ballooning of prices for such commodities. In such cases the enormous revenues governments receive are not so much a sign of the effectiveness of the political system as of purely economic advantages that make it possible for them to gather substantial revenues in spite of poor political performance.

Controls, then, were essential, and we attempted to adjust for tax revenues derived either from the mining share of the GNP or from exports. We found, however, that only the mining share of the GNP seemed to affect the results. We think the reason adjusting for exports as a share of GNP failed to prove an effective control is that, because the only data available are those for total exports, it proved impossible to separate traditional economies (those with a commercial agricultural sector that, though tied to the international market, is separate from the indigenous economic and social systems) exporting solely agricultural commodities from modern nations exporting both industrial and agricultural commodities. But, of course, the whole point of controlling for exports was to distinguish nations with dual economies from modern economic systems. Data on total exports did not, then, do the job. As noted, however, controlling for revenues derived from mining worked. Adjustments for mining revenues were carried out in such a way as to increase or decrease the maximum according to advantages or disadvantages in national tax bases as a result of mineral possessions:[8]

> Adjusted maximum extraction ratio = maximum extraction ratio in war × (1 + [mineral production]/GDP − [mean mineral production]/GDP)

where the maximum extraction ratio in war is 0.55 of GDP for developed nations and 0.40 for developing nations.

As a result of this adjustment, if a nation produced more or less than the average of the production of all nations in the sample, that amount was added to or subtracted from the maximum extraction level. This adjustment proved important in the case of developing countries with vast mineral resources.

Political Costs

Let us now turn to the last element in the model. The concept of political costs is critical to the working of the model, and we discussed this concept at some length in the preceding chapter. Political costs are the resources required to build up the repressive mechanism of the state (the armies and the police forces), the extractive mechanism of the state (the bureaucracies), the mobilizing institutions (the political parties), and the fund of resources necessary to co-opt the remaining resistance to the central authorities emanating from various quarters of the society. Such resistance, one will recall, takes the form of open violence and warfare at the beginning of the process of state building and continues in a more peaceful but no less stubborn manner once economic development has begun in earnest.

We measure political costs by taking the difference between the adjusted maximum quantity of resources a country is expected to collect and the amount of adjusted revenues actually collected.

Political costs = [adjusted maximum extraction ratio − adjusted tax ratio] × 100

The key to the model is rooted in this comparison. The reason we take the gap between these two figures to reflect political costs lies in our answer to the following question: Why is it that most nations, most of the time, do not achieve the maximum possible level of taxation? The reason is not that they do not want to. As we explained when we discussed our adjustments of the data we used in analyzing political performance, we have already taken into account what governments give back as well as what they extract from their societies. It is our view, rather, that structural components play the dominant role in setting limits. Our model rests on the assumption—one we believe is valid—that all political leaders of whatever stripe will try to extract all the resources they can, given what they are trying to do. If they fail to collect all they need to carry out their plans, it is because they cannot: Either because they do not have the tools to impose their will or because the opposition is too strong, they do not possess the wherewithal to meet the political price they must pay to reach the maximum.

Such an interpretation finds strong support in the case of currently developed countries. Why do they fail to reach the maximum level of extraction estimated for them? The problem is certainly not economic; developed nations have a good deal of surplus wealth that government could tap. Yet the fact remains that this wealth is not tapped, and the governments of these countries often are in serious fiscal trouble. The answer obviously is that there are political obstacles to raising the funds they require, obstacles they cannot surmount. Or take the opposite angle of vision on the problem. How was North Vietnam able to extract almost half the gross national product from its population during the Vietnam War? It was certainly not because the Vietnamese had great wealth to spare their government, for, as we have already indicated, the per capita product of North Vietnam during the war was only about one hundred dollars a year.

A number of points need to be noted at this juncture. The measure of political costs used here bears almost exclusively on *political* behavior. Consequently, quite apart from serving as an indicator of government capacity, it permits us to circumvent the problem that arises because taxes result from the combined operation of the economic and political subsystems. If all one has to work with are revenue totals, one cannot disentangle the respective contributions of the political and economic sectors to total government resources—a circumstance that, for obvious reasons, makes it difficult to arrive at a correct assessment of government performance.

Now consider. The estimate of the maximum level of taxation countries can be expected to reach under ideal conditions has been obtained by using as a guide the taxation performance of combatants locked in mortal combat in total war. But war is a political phenomenon, not an economic one, and during hostilities—whatever part they may have played in initiating them—economic interests have to take a backseat. Moreover, the maximum has already been adjusted to correct for differences in the tax base. Therefore the method by which we arrive at the maximum is free of economic considerations.

The same cannot be said of our index of actual political performance. In devising our measure of political capacity, we have advanced the hypothesis that, if countries fail to reach the maximum level of taxation we have estimated they ought to achieve under ideal conditions, it is because there are political obstacles to their doing so: the *political* costs involved in extracting resources are too high. Because we use total tax collection, which is a function of economic and political factors, as the subtrahend in the subtraction that gives us our index of political costs, the operation of the economic system plays only a very peripheral role in this measure. Thus a substantial portion of the effect of politics remains commingled with economic effects in a way that leads us to underestimate the political factors, since part of these factors —the part included in actual taxation—are not included in our measure of political costs. How much of the political effect is embedded in such measures as GNP is impossible to tell at present. But we submit that the amount is indeed substantial. This comment should be kept in mind when we examine the results of our analysis. Those results portray only the effect on vital rates exerted by that portion of the political system that we have succeeded in disentangling from nonpolitical influences.

As the second point to be made at this juncture, we suggest that there is another way of thinking about political costs and political capacity. The reader may think of political costs in terms of the flexibility or freedom a government enjoys: not so much in terms of the resources a government has already obtained but rather of how easy or difficult it is for it to obtain *new* resources. This is an old problem, often debated. Does the very rich man whose income is fully committed to creditors, wife, and profligate children have any financial power? Or, more to the point, compare once again the United States and Sweden. The Swedish government taxes proportionately far more heavily than the American government. But Swedish leaders are less free than American leaders in their allocation of resources. They have little choice about how resources are to be spent, since what they collect is already committed to specific programs; and because they tax so heavily, it is extremely difficult to increase their revenue. Is it, then, incorrect to think of the United States government as being more capable than its Swedish counterpart on the grounds that, even though the latter succeeds in raising greater sums in taxes, the former has more flexibility in undertaking new programs?

It should be clear, however, that this focus—not on what governments do with the resources at their disposal, but rather on how easy or difficult they find it to raise *new* resources—has already been implicitly included in our estimate of political costs. When all is said and done, the costs involved in raising resources and the degree of choice governments exercise in initiating new programs constitute two sides of the same coin, and they are of course inversely related to each other. For when the political costs incurred in collecting additional taxes are high, the range of options open to governments will be correspondingly narrow and, naturally enough, as costs come down, the range of options widens accordingly. The forces over which governments must prevail in gathering resources are the same forces they must contend with in deciding how those resources are to be used. Their success in one area of performance can consequently be accurately inferred from the other.

One final point. In the preceding chapter we suggested that costs were not uniformly distributed across all countries at any one time or across the different stages through which each single country passes along the entire developmental continuum. We argued, in other words, that political costs vary from one nation to another and also, within the experience of a single nation, from one phase in the process of development to another. Again, given our explanation of the forces underlying the growth of the political apparatus of the state, political costs should be high at the beginning of the trajectory of political development, low in the middle, and high once more in the stage of political maturity, at the end of the shift from underdeveloped to developed status. The results of the empirical analysis will indeed show that there is substantial variation in the political costs paid by nations at different stages of the developmental process, and this variation displays the curvilinearity our theoretical structure leads us to expect.

Now, it is our hunch that this curvilinearity in the structure of costs reflects the fact that the costs of extracting resources vary at the margins across the developmental process. Clearly, calculating such marginal political costs would be immensely useful, but unfortunately no good procedure yet exists for determining the marginal costs of political extraction incurred by each individual nation at each point in the developmental process. What is possible, however, as the reader will see in the analysis to follow, is a calculus that, though far less precise than we might wish, will do for the moment. It is our view that the mean of the costs incurred by nations at each level of development—displayed in table 2 (p. 93)—do indeed suggest the curvilinearity which should be present in the costs structure. We assume that underdeveloped countries are prevented from moving up the developmental ladder to the level of developing nations by the high marginal costs involved in extracting the resources needed for such an ascent. On the other hand, it is the lower costs incurred at the margin that permit nations in the developing category to move so much faster in extracting resources, thus enabling them to climb the ladder of development with much greater ease. Finally, it is owing to a new rise in marginal costs that governments at the developed level find it so difficult to expand their capacity to extract resources in spite of the immense wealth economic development has brought them.

The averages in table 2 (p. 93) describe a curve following just this sort of line.

Conclusion

Let us review very briefly the model proposed in these pages. We establish a maximum possible level of taxation for developing and for developed countries. The figures are 40 percent of GDP for developing countries and 55 percent for developed countries. We index the level of political capacity reached by taking the fraction of total taxes over GDP. After the maximum and taxes are adjusted on the side of expenditures for policy preferences and on the supply side for economic differences in the tax base, we subtract the adjusted taxes from the adjusted maximum. This is the estimate of political costs we shall use in our analysis as the measure of the independent variable, political development.

The Socioeconomic and Demographic Variables

While we may have chosen to explore the question of population growth from a somewhat new perspective, we do not seek to recast the fundamental macrolevel framework painstakingly constructed by other investigators. Rather, as we have indicated throughout this volume, we accept the basic traditional view of the relation between economic and sociocultural factors on the one side and vital rates on the other even as we recognize the need to specify the precise nature of this relation, which has given rise to somewhat varying models propounded by diverse investigators, each bringing to the task not only different disciplinary perspectives but different data bases and personal preconceptions.

Our purpose is instead to contribute to the overall picture of the determinants of vital rates by presenting our findings on what we contend is a significant, yet till now largely overlooked and unexplored, factor in demographic behavior. We have said that the main factors considered by investigators from other disciplines are, if not macrolevel determinants, then at least correlates of vital rates. The numerous, often imaginative and sophisticated approaches applied in exploring these factors demonstrate at the very least the incontrovertibly strong associations between vital rates and such variables as income, education, health status, and cultural and religious background. In introducing the variable of political capacity, however, we suggest that we shall not merely improve the predictive capacity of earlier models, but also elucidate more precisely the workings of these other previously observed relationships, thus improving the specification and prehension of earlier models.

We have just described how we constructed our measure of change and growth in the political system. The transformation of the political system is, however, only one of the structural changes that we argue play a role in bringing down vital rates in the demographic transition. Other factors are also important causes of the decrease: education, particularly the education of women, urbanization, rises in income, technical innovations in medical science and sanitation, cultural attitudes toward children all have been shown to contribute to the downward movement of vital rates once social and economic modernization has taken place. Indeed, such factors are the very core of what has been called development. But how does one combine all these factors and go about introducing them into an overall model in order to test our central hypothesis regarding the contribution of political development to decreases in births and deaths?

Two alternative ways of dealing with this problem were clearly open. We could develop a sophisticated model that would consider all contending variables concurrently, then determine the specific effect of political change within this overall context. This was the complex way to go. We did not adopt this approach for two main reasons. The socioeconomic variables listed above are known to be highly correlated with one another and to reflect similar effects. It was not necessary, therefore, to develop a very complex model incorporating them all individually, for the most inclusive could serve as an indicator of all the rest. The second reason for not choosing this approach was that many of the steps required could not be performed. Had we included individually all the different socioeconomic variables involved, we would ultimately have had to identify the various components of the political system that we believe determine government capacity as systems advanced from nondeveloped to developed status, suggest indicators for each of the components we would use, and then obtain the data necessary to estimate these indicators. But, as we have had frequent occasion to note, given the current state of the art of measuring political development, this proved impossible. As the reader is well aware, we have succeeded in measuring political growth and development for this effort only indirectly.

Thus we chose the other alternative, which consists of using a single measure—but the most encompassing possible—as a summary of all the various social and economic changes affecting vital rates and then determining whether adding the measure of political costs would add substantially to the overall power of the model. Not surprisingly, per capita total product was chosen as the single most powerful indicator of economic and social change. And with good reason. It is well accepted that per capita product is an all-inclusive variable reflecting the effect of all of the various social and economic factors—for example, urbanization, industrialization, education—that we would have had to measure directly had we chosen the complex model described above. We were reassured that this strategy was indeed correct when we compared the behavior of the political variable with that of the different economic and social factors mentioned earlier and found, as others had, that the socioeconomic factors were highly correlated with one another while the relation between them and the political variable was weak.[9] Indeed, the highest correlation was between per capita product and the political measure. The simplicity of this model, moreover, gave us a clear advantage. The relation between our dependent and independent variables, should there prove to be one, would stand out boldly, and of course the opposite would also be true: if no relation were there, and our expectations were not sustained by the analysis, this too would be readily apparent.

We were of course aware of the difficulties of using per capita product as an index.[10] Per capita product is not a perfect indicator of the reality we wish to index, and the many transformations of foreign currencies into current and constant dollars made distortions in our data inevitable. Clearly, had the necessary data been available, the use of a nonmonetary index would have been preferable. Even then, however, distortions would have arisen in any comparison across time, for there would have been no way to adjust for changes in technology affecting the composition of goods produced. It was far from a perfect solution, but we consoled ourselves that the authors of the World Bank data on which we relied had made a strong attempt to minimize these distortions. Finally, we knew that whatever error one had to contend with on the economic side of our model would be smaller than the error contained in our political variable. It therefore made good sense to us to concentrate on minimizing distortions where we knew the error would be larger.

The Demographic Variables

The last step in preparing our analysis was measuring the vital rates we wished to use as the dependent variable. Here we encountered no real difficulties. Not surprisingly, we chose crude birth and death rates as the central indicators. Such rates are obtained by counting the number of children born and the number of deaths occurring in a given year, dividing the results by the total midyear population, and multiplying the quotient by one thousand.

Though other, less gross measures of vital rates could have been used, the reasons for using crude rates were compelling. The data for crude rates were more readily available than those for more refined indicators, and when one attempts cross-national, cross-temporal analysis the availability of data is often a deciding factor in the choice of research strategies. Crude rates, moreover, are the ones political leaders themselves use in their decisions on demographic and related matters. But the principal reason for using crude rates was our uncertainty whether the level of analysis at which a large number of constraints compelled us to operate justified utilizing more sophisticated demographic indicators.

There are, of course, limitations in the data we used. The most important of these arises because, owing to vast differences in the age structures of different populations, crude figures substantially misrepresent vital rates in cross-national comparisons. How distortions may come about can easily be imagined. In a rapidly growing population, for example, the mortality rate is underestimated because there are large numbers of young people; conversely, the fertility rate is overestimated owing to the relatively large number of women of reproductive age. These effects are important when we compare vital rates across nations or attempt to evaluate the behavior of one rapidly changing population over a period of time. One finds, for instance, that the unadjusted crude death rate for Greece in 1970 is lower than that for Germany even though Germany enjoys far greater socioeconomic development. Similarly, using unadjusted data, one discovers that, since 1950, the mortality rate in Germany is increasing rather than decreasing, a finding that again belies the fundamental demographic reality as indicated by the state of socioeconomic development. These patterns are a direct result of differences in the structure and changes in the age composition of the population concerned, differences and changes that are not taken into account in calculating crude vital rates and are therefore patent distortions of relative fertility and mortality levels and of the dynamic transformations at work.

Because age structures affect mortality and fertility in different ways, we devised two separate adjustments to minimize the distortions in question and achieve the compatibility our design required. We used a fairly orthodox standardization procedure to adjust the data relating to mortality in order to eliminate the effects of variation in age structure.[11] Using a standard population, we computed what the crude rates would be if age structures did not vary across countries. For each time point, the age-specific mortality rate of a given country was multiplied by the equivalent age-specific population in a standard population. The adjusted crude death rate was obtained by multiplying a ratio between the cumulative total mortality across age groups in the standard population and the size of the standard population. The population of England and Wales in 1960 was the standard used throughout. All adjustments were made at five-year intervals. For most developed nations, this process simply entailed collecting readily available age-specific mortality rates to standardize the crude data directly.

For developing nations and a few time points in the experience of developed countries, however, this direct approach was not feasible. Data on age-specific mortality rates are sporadic and of low quality. Of necessity, therefore, estimates were derived of age-standardized mortality rates, using male life expectancy at birth in conjunction with the Western male family of the Coale-Demeny model life tables. These estimates, in turn, were used to obtain adjusted crude death rates following the same procedure described for developed nations.

It should be obvious that the choice of a particular life table is arbitrary and that relying on the male population alone distorts the adjustments. More important, the use of life-table techniques assumes a stable population with a stable vital rate over a long period. This assumption is seriously violated in the case of many, perhaps most, of the developing nations. For countries that have experienced rapid declines in mortality over the period studied, the bias introduced may be considerable. We nevertheless felt that, given the direction and the extent of the adjustments made, these effects were not great enough to affect the analysis. But further study clearly will lead to more accurate and effective adjustments in the future.

Let us now consider birthrates. The objective here was again to eliminate variations in birthrates introduced by age structures.[12] But whereas in the adjustments of crude death rates we possessed an orthodox procedure for standardizing the data, no such procedure was readily available for standardizing fertility rates. We were eager to reduce the differential effect of the proportion of couples of childbearing age in a given population, a number that in a comparatively young population will unduly increase, and in an old one unduly depress, fertility rates. To this end, we established at five-year intervals the ratio between the number of women ages fifteen to forty-four in each nation in the study and the same group in the standard population. Again the standard was England and Wales in 1960. The adjusted crude birthrate was obtained by multiplying this ratio by the original crude rates.

As with mortality rates, it was not possible to control fully for all the effects of changes in vital rates. Nevertheless, the adjusted birthrate behaved as expected. Absolute levels of fertility were reduced except in a few highly developed societies. Further, in relatively young populations the standardization required was strong, while in relatively old populations the necessary adjustments were slight. There is good reason to believe that the gross adjustments we desired have been achieved.

Conclusion

We have now discussed the theory, data, and procedures involved in preparing the independent and dependent variables for the experiment we wished to carry out. We have explained in detail how we constructed our models of political development, our choice of the measure to be used, and why per capita GNP was used to represent the other socioeconomic factors known to influence vital rates. We have also given a detailed explanation of the steps we followed in adjusting vital rates and the reasons these steps had to be taken. The goal of the experiment, let us repeat, is to test whether the massive institutional transformation known as "political development" has, as we suppose, a decided effect on the fertility and mortality of national populations.

Now, at last, let us turn to the analysis.

4 The Empirical Analysis

Introduction

We have already discussed how our measures of extractive capacity and political costs were constructed and the steps we undertook to prepare the data relating to fertility and mortality rates, the dependent variables in our experiment. We should, however, take this opportunity to recall why we allege that a connection exists between political capacity and vital rates and why we believe the relation is inverse. Though we have stated our reasons in chapters 1 and 2, they need at least brief mention here.

We think that with the expansion of the political system governmental power inevitably intrudes into people's lives, and that this intrusion just as inevitably brings profound alterations in patterns of births and deaths. Instances of government interventions that prevent deaths are too numerous to mention. Law and order, rules ensuring proper nutrition, sanitary and medical programs, safety precautions in the workplace, regulations assuring orderly economic and social exchanges, safety standards for travel, and so on and so forth: there is practically no end to the ways government power is used to save lives. Nor is resistance to intrusions of this kind very strong, since the advantage of trading "liberty" for additional years of life is clear to all. But government intrusion affects birthrates as well. Government rules can make having and rearing children costlier, make potential parents more aware of the costs involved, and provide alternatives to bearing children. And all this, not surprisingly, ceteris paribus, can turn people away from having larger families.

The general relation we postulate is clear enough. Testing our hypothesis, however, requires several steps, and their enumeration provides the table of contents for this chapter. We must explain in detail the nature of the data to be used, the characteristics of the sample, and the period the analysis covers. We must also describe the models used to carry out the analysis, transform the theoretical propositions outlined at length in chapters 1 and 2 into operational hypotheses, and, finally, give the results we obtained. So as not to bore the reader, we shall relegate to the appendixes the detailed documentation of the steps performed along the way, concentrating in the text only on the principal points under discussion.

The Time Frame of the Study

All the data in the analysis are drawn from the period 1950 to 1975. Though the process under examination extends in almost every case, from start to finish, over one hundred years or more, the reader should not find it surprising that there is only a thin slice of time available for empirical study. In the world of cross-national fiscal and national account data, recorded history begins in the 1950s. For any period before that one has to work with unreliable estimates, and the gaps in the data are huge. So far as demographic data are concerned, our series does not really begin at the stage of high potential growth when, according to the transition theory, both death rates and birthrates should be very high. By 1950, even in the least economically developed countries, most death rates have begun to fall even though birthrates have remained high. Roughly, then, the earliest data on vital rates included in the series relate to the beginning of the phase of transitional growth, that is, the second of the three stages described in the demographic transition theory.[1]

Here an aside is necessary regarding the availability of data. In the main, with the exception of a few countries, economic and fiscal data of the quality necessary do not exist for dates earlier than 1950. Series recording vital rates do exist for a few European countries going back to the late nineteenth century and in a few cases much earlier still. Such longer series are not available, however, for enough countries to permit the kind of analysis we want to attempt here. In any event they cannot be used unless series of equal length can be developed for the fiscal data, which is highly unlikely. There is, of course, one way to obtain demographic, economic, and fiscal series long enough for the kind of analysis we wish to carry out. One could simply not pursue the research now but wait until the countries currently undergoing the transition from underdevelopment to development complete their developmental trajectories. Only then would we have in hand, for all of the segments composing the transition, the demographic and socioeconomic data needed to capture the true dynamic of the relationship between the economic, political, and demographic changes we wish to explain. Then it would no longer be necessary to use a cross-sectional research design to gain a glimpse of this historical dynamic. But this will not be possible for a long time to come; the task will fall to others coming after us, and then, perhaps, the inquiry only imperfectly begun here will be brought to a proper conclusion. For the moment, however, we are left with the necessity of inferring the historical dynamic at the root of change in vital rates from cross-sectional data derived for a very short period. As the reader will remember, this same problem faced the authors of the demographic transition theory.

Still, things are not all bad. Note that the brief time for which data are available happens to be the best possible period for this kind of analysis. For it is precisely after World War II that one finds the greatest differences in political expansion and effectiveness between nations, with minimal changes occurring in those socioeconomic patterns that previous analyses have regarded as the primary cause of declines in vital rates. This state of affairs immensely simplifies the construction of our experiment, for it builds into our design a kind of natural control for the effects of political change on vital rates.

The Sample

The second matter to consider here is the composition of the sample of nations whose demographic behavior furnished the data for the dependent variable in our experiment. Obviously it was our purpose to include as many countries as possible. But some nations had to be left out, and the reader should be told which were omitted and why.

All nations of less than a million inhabitants were excluded from the sample. On that list were all of the lilliputian city-states like Monaco and Liechtenstein. These miniature states are totally dependent for their existence on the surrounding systems, and there is therefore no way to index their political capacity properly. A second set of nations we eliminated were the communist countries, because, given their totally centralized economic systems, there is as yet no way to measure their political capacity using fiscal indicators and therefore no way to estimate the effect of their political systems on the vital rates of their populations. From our point of view this was highly regrettable, because there is good reason to suspect that it is precisely in these countries that the political system has had, both directly and indirectly, the most pronounced depressive effect on vital rates.

A third set of countries was left out of our final sample because there were insufficient data either for the socioeconomic variables required to establish indicators of the political costs of extracting resources or for indexes of demographic behavior. As we noted a moment ago, the lack of data is always a major problem for researchers performing cross-national analyses. As one would expect, since the quality of national statistics itself is a good indicator of socioeconomic and political development, we had good data for developed countries for each year in the series, but there were gaps in the data for developing countries. Thus, as one went down the developmental ladder one began to run into Latin American, Asian, and African states that could enter our sample only for short periods rather than for the entire length of the series. Many of these countries, of course, were colonies during some portion of the period under consideration, and we excluded all colonial possessions, since it is clearly impossible to estimate political capacity when the system does not possess an independent government. But the countries in question do appear in our sample the moment they gain independence.[2]

Division of the Sample

We outlined in chapter 1 the general relation we think exists between politics and vital rates. In choosing a model that would be

able to capture this relation, we had to meet an essential require-
ment. It was necessary, first of all, that the model should permit us
to estimate the specific effects of political development on vital
rates by controlling for the powerful influence socioeconomic
change exerts on fertility and mortality. As we noted earlier, one
cannot read out the effect of economic influences completely,
because per capita GNP, the most parsimonious measure of
economic and social behavior available for large-scale cross-
national comparisons, reflects a combination of social and political
as well as economic factors. We discussed at length in chapter 3
how we got around the difficulties this poses by using a measure of
political costs rather than a measure of actual extractive capacity
itself, thus arming ourselves with an estimate of taxation in which
the respective contributions of the political and economic systems
were much less commingled. Yet since GNP and our measure of
capacity are still related, we decided to control for the former one
more time. As we shall argue later, we have reason to believe that
the effect of political capacity varies across levels of economic
development. Therefore we grouped the countries in the sample
into sets of underdeveloped, developing, and developed nations.

Let us now explain very briefly just how these groupings were
established. The *nondeveloped* world was divided into two groups,
and a third group was composed entirely of OECD nations.
Different rules were applied in composing the nondeveloped and
developed groups. Per capita income was the yardstick used in
dividing the countries in the nondeveloped world into two groups.
The underdeveloped group was composed of the poorest countries
in the nondeveloped world, with per capita products in the first to
the fiftieth percentile for any one year in the series; the developing
group was composed of all nations with per capita products in the
fifty-first to the one hundredth percentile for any one year in the
series.

It was important to redivide our sample every year in case some
countries moved from one group to the other, and many of them
did. Had we divided the countries in the study only once for the
entire period, we would have seriously biased our sample by
unduly reducing the representation of poorer countries, for two
reasons. First, in the decade 1950–60 a large number of the
countries that were later to fill the ranks of the underdeveloped
and developing categories were still colonies, and therefore the

total sample of countries for which data were available would have contained a higher proportion of developed nations than otherwise. Second, over the entire period covered in this analysis, there was a substantial increase in the wealth of all nations, including those in the nondeveloped world.

The criterion by which nations were assigned to the category of developed countries differed from that used in grouping the nations of the nondeveloped world. We simply decided to include in the developed group all of the OECD countries. The yardstick of per capita GNP was not used as a measure of selection in this case, for good reason.

One should keep in mind that per capita product was used as an index of development because it correlates very highly with other factors—education, urbanization, status of women, modes of production, and so forth—that are themselves the real forces behind the movement of vital rates. Per capita product is not, however, a good indicator for developed countries during one segment of the period covered by our analysis. Particularly in the decade after World War II, most of the nations of Western Europe, making up the largest fraction of the developed world, suffered severe economic depression as a result of the death and destruction caused by the war. Levels of per capita product in many Western European countries were therefore lower in the late forties and fifties than the per capita product of many developing countries during the sixties and seventies. Clearly, for many Western European nations these temporarily low per capita products provide poor indicators of levels of education, technology, type of social structure, and so on, factors essential to our analysis. We accordingly decided to compensate for this possibly serious distortion by including in the category of developed countries all the members of the OECD group. This offered a defensible and simple way out of our dilemma. But the reader should remember that this also creates problems of its own, inasmuch as it leads us to include in the category of the developed world countries such as Spain, Greece, and Portugal that, for a major portion of the period covered by this analysis, would not have been included on the basis of their economic performance.

This, then, was the procedure we used to group the sample of countries into our three categories. As we have said before, though we made every effort to disentangle political from economic factors, we were not entirely successful. Nevertheless, we have managed to keep the correlations low for the entire sample as well as for each stratum of economic development. This is shown in table 1.

Table 1
Correlation of Economic and Political Variables:
Political Capacity as Expressed by Political Costs

	Underdeveloped	Developing	Developed	Total Sample
Per capita GNP	−.04	−.36	−.32	−.13
N	726	729	413	1,886

One final point. The reader will recall that, in chapter 2, we showed why and how our measure of the political costs of extracting resources, our index of the change undergone by political systems under conditions of development, was expected to behave. We hypothesized that it should vary across levels of development in the following fashion. At the beginning of the process of state construction, the marginal political costs involved in expanding the extraction of the growing amounts of human and material resources required should be high. In the middle of the state-building process these costs should reach their lowest point. But once the state structure has been fully constructed and the political system had fully expanded, costs should rise again to a very high level. As we noted in chapter 2, the curvilinearity of the pattern described by the evolution of political costs offers a critical piece of information about the nature of the process of state construction and the massive expansion through which the political system passes in achieving its mature form and size. And our expectation that the pattern should be curvilinear is indeed fully borne out by our data on the political costs encountered by the countries in our sample, spread out along developmental lines. The mean for each group is presented in table 2.

Table 2 gives a critical piece of information. The means of the distribution of the political costs of extracting resources for each of the groups in table 2 describe the anticipated curvilinear structure only faintly. But by breaking the total sample down into economic groups finer than simply underdeveloped, developing, and developed, we discovered a more pronounced curvilinear structure. Still, it is our view that the averages shown provide a first

Table 2
Structure of Marginal Political Costs

	Underdeveloped		Developing		Developed	
	$\overline{X}$	SD	$\overline{X}$	SD	$\overline{X}$	SD
Means of political capacity as expressed by political costs	27.1	4.9	25.4	6.1	31.1	5.1
N	726		729		413	

Note: Political costs reach a maximum at zero.

indication of the marginal costs of extracting resources at each level of development. And, as predicted, underdeveloped and developed countries have higher relative political costs than developing countries.

An additional point needs to be made regarding this table. There are two important gaps in our sample of countries. The costs of extraction in group 1 appear lower at the very beginning of state construction than they probably are in fact because we have no countries in our series just entering on the process of state building. All the countries in the world had by 1950 already traveled some distance beyond this initial point.[3] This is precisely the same situation we have found on the demographic side of our analysis. There too, even in the most economically underdeveloped countries, death rates had already begun to fall by the start of the period covered in our study, and we therefore judged the population to be in the initial phase of stage 2 of the demographic transition rather than in stage 1. The second important gap in our sample of countries appears between groups 2 and 3. As table 2 shows, the difference in means between the set of developing countries and the set of developed countries is sharp. But the impression this conveys of pronounced discontinuity between the two groups is fundamentally misleading and reflects the fact that a number of countries that had already reached a point halfway between developing and fully developed status are missing from our sample. The countries in question are for the most part the communist countries of Eastern Europe: Hungary, Poland, Czechoslovakia, East Germany, and so forth. Had it been possible to add these nations to our sample, they would have joined countries like Portugal, Spain, Argentina, and Brazil in making up the set of nations midway between developing and developed status, and the great gap between group 2 and group 3 would have been filled. In short, had we had available for our sample both nations at the very beginning of the process of development and also nations midway between developing and developed status, a very smooth curvilinear structure would no doubt have appeared. Be that as it may, the missing data do not permit us to make breakdowns beyond those we have already made here.[4]

Operational Hypotheses

Let us repeat once more in detail what we expect the relation between political costs and vital rates to be. In trying to set this down we have to keep in mind the connection between this relation and shifts in political and economic levels.

We begin with birthrates. The reader will recall that in chapter 2, when presenting the theoretical model of the link between the political and demographic transitions, we argued that the political costs of extracting resources are positively related to birthrates during the early and middle stages of economic development. This is so because, at these stages, political costs and extractive capacity are inversely related: political costs decrease, allowing extractive capacity to increase. Thus, in the early and middle stages of development a decrease in political costs will be associated with a reduction in birthrates via an increase in extractive capacity. Since it is reasonable to expect that economic progress lends greater strength to extractive capacity, we should expect that, at middle levels of development, a decrease in costs will be associated with a sharper fall in birthrates than at earlier stages.

The relation between political costs, extractive capacity, and birthrates is quite different, however, at higher levels of economic development. At these levels political capacity is at its height. But so are political costs. This means that political capacity will tend to stabilize at high levels of development, since it is unlikely that the political system will go into a decline at this stage, while the growing difficulty in acquiring resources practically rules out further government expansion. Thus, at these higher levels, political costs will be on the rise while political capacity will remain constant. For a short period, therefore, political costs will no longer reflect political capacity. After a time, however, as political capacity levels off, so will political costs. Since we have reason to believe political capacity will remain constant, we also expect fertility levels to remain constant. In that case political costs will show almost no effect on birthrates.

Our central hypothesis, then, is that we shall find political capacity, as expressed in the costs of extracting resources, having a steadily increasing influence on fertility as nations rise from underdeveloped to developing status. To this point political development acts as a powerful accelerator of the fall of vital rates. After this point there should be little or no impact. And we shall look in particular at the effects of the strength of the relation between political costs and fertility for the entire sample of countries, for developing and underdeveloped countries alone, and, finally, for the developed groups.

Results

To test our hypotheses, we have postulated a linear model[5] that yields three regressions corresponding to the three levels of development. These are presented in table 3.

Table 3
The Birthrates Equations: Effect of Political Capacity as Expressed by Political Costs for Each Level of Economic Development
(y = Birthrates, x = Political Costs)

Underdeveloped: $y = 34 + .28x$
Developing: $y = 22 + .63x$
Developed: $y = 15 + .07x$
$N = 1,868$
$R^2 = .68$ (R^2 for GNP/population alone = .63)

The results shown in table 3 fully meet our expectations concerning the differences we should find in the strength of the relation between political costs and fertility at the various levels of economic development. The coefficients .28, .63 and .07 derived for the underdeveloped, developing, and developed groups show clearly that political growth has a good deal of influence on the birthrates of populations of underdeveloped nations and exerts a very powerful influence in developing countries. The more than doubling of the size of the coefficients when we pass from underdeveloped to developing countries confirms our suspicion that the effect of political capacity is much stronger in the latter. Again, as we also expected, political growth seems to have no effect on crude birthrates at the developed level, for the simple reason that further political expansion at this stage is very difficult to bring about since the marginal costs of doing so are terribly high. And given that once nations reach full maturity fertility levels are already very low, any further decrease would be exceedingly unlikely even if mature political systems could easily be expanded.

Our results require another word of comment and additional analysis. Since our categories, based on per capita GNP, were constructed somewhat arbitrarily and contain much variation, one could argue that the coefficients derived for the political costs of extracting resources reflect an undue constraint of the variance in GNP found within each of the three groups of nations more than they express the impact of the political variable with which we are specifically concerned. To see if this was so, we allowed per capita GNP to vary within each level of economic development.[6] We obtained the three regressions set forth in table 4.

Table 4
The Full Model for Birth Rates: Effect of per Capita GNP and Political Capacity as Expressed by Political Costs for Each Level of Economic Development
(y = Birthrates, x = Costs, z = GNP/Population)

Underdeveloped: $y = 32 + .27x + .01z$
Developing: $y = 20 + .84x - .00z$
Developed: $y = 20 + .00x - .00z$
$N = 1,808$
$R^2 = .72$ (R^2 for GNP/population alone $= .65$)

The least-squares estimates shown in table 4 clearly indicate that, even if we allow per capita product to vary within each level of development, we still obtain results very similar to the ones in table 3. Thus the suspicion that at least some of the effects we attribute to political growth may be nothing more than an artifact of the constraints imposed by our model seems unfounded.

As table 4 shows, political costs add 7 percent to the variance in fertility rates explained by GNP. The reader should not forget, however, something that has been a constant refrain through major portions of this book. Per capita GNP is an all-encompassing variable. Since it is correlated with political costs, it probably robs that factor of some of the variance explained by the latter. Furthermore, the coefficient of determination for the general model is an "average" of the coefficients of determination we would obtain by running separate regressions for each level of economic development. When we run these, the differences between the R^2s obtained by regressing fertility on both per capita GNP and political costs and those obtained by regressing it on per capita GNP alone clearly indicate that the measure of political costs adds a considerable amount to the variance in fertility explained by per capita GNP. This is seen in table 5.

Table 5
Regression of Birthrates on per Capita GNP and Political Capacity as
Expressed by Political Costs for Each Level of Development

	Coefficients for Underdeveloped ($N = 726$)	Coefficients for Developing ($N = 729$)	Coefficients for Developed ($N = 413$)
Per capita GNP	.01	.00	.00
Political costs	.28	.84	.00
R_1^2	.12	.27	.09
Per capita GNP alone	.01	.00	.00
R_2^2	.05	.03	.09
$R_1^2 - R_2^2$	.07	.24	.00

All these findings concerning the relation between economic development, political costs, and birthrates can be neatly seen in the three-dimensional figure below (fig. 9).

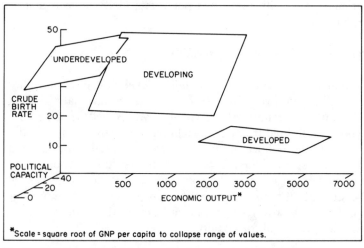

Fig. 9. Relation of birthrates to political costs and wealth, 1950–75.

In figure 9 economic improvements in underdeveloped countries vitiate fertility reductions somewhat owing to political factors. In the group of developing countries both economic and political factors pull together to reduce fertility. And, as expected, there are no effects in the developed group. As we noted earlier, the sharp discontinuity between developing and developed groups is due to deficiencies in the sample.

As a final point, we take one more step in our analysis of birthrates. If we concentrate entirely on the nondeveloped world, excluding the OECD countries, and replicate the analysis using our second model, we obtain added and dramatic confirmation that it is politics rather than economic development that leads to decreases in rates of fertility in the nondeveloped world. The full results of this analysis are shown in table 6.

Table 6
Effects of GNP/Population and Political Costs
on Birthrates of Underdeveloped and Developing Nations
(y = Birthrates, x = Political Costs, z = GNP/Population)

Underdeveloped: $y = 32 + .28x + .01z$
Developing: $y = 21 + .84x - .00z$
$R^2 = .29$ (GNP/population alone, $R^2 = .10$)
$N = 1,455$

In this case political costs explain almost 20 percent of the variance in fertility over what per capita GNP alone is able to explain.

Political Development and Mortality

In analyzing the effects of political development on mortality, we shall repeat every step we have taken in our analysis of the effects of political growth on fertility. We expect the same basic hypothesis to hold true for mortality as for fertility; namely, that the lower the political costs, the greater the reduction in death rates. But again, although we expect the relation between death rates and political costs to be positive in every case, we also expect the strength of the relation to vary across levels of development. We do not, however, expect to find exactly the same pattern of variation we found for fertility.

Mortality responds to increases in political capacity much more rapidly than does fertility. This means that the amount of mortality to be reduced will decrease much more rapidly as economic development progresses. One should expect to find, therefore, that the greatest effect of political development occurs at earlier stages of development than in the case of fertility. Using the same general model employed to study the effects of politics on fertility, the least-squares estimates shown in table 7 indicate that the effect of political costs is greatest at the first level, continues to descend rapidly as we move to developing countries, and almost vanishes as we move from the developing to the developed world. This is precisely what we expected.

Table 7
The Death Rates Equations: Effect of Political Capacity as Expressed by Political Costs for Each Level of Economic Development
(Y = **Death Rates,** x = **Political Costs**)

Underdeveloped: $Y = 17 + .41x$
Developing: $\quad Y = 13 + .24x$
Developed: $\quad\ Y = \ 8 + .09x$
$N = 1,868$
$R^2 = .68$ (for GNP/population alone $R^2 = .64$)

We explained earlier why we hypothesize that political growth will have its strongest effects on mortality at that point where the political system is admittedly weak and expansion is accordingly difficult to bring about. There is no need to go over this ground again. But we should remind the reader that the initial decreases in death rates are the consequence of the increased order and security that result from the initial creation of a national army and a central bureaucracy, the first steps in establishing a modern state. So it should not come as a surprise that political growth begins to push death rates downward precisely at that point in the process of state construction where central political institutions are beginning to emerge and while the political costs involved are still very high.

Here let us point out once again that, since our categories based on per capita GNP were constructed somewhat arbitrarily, one might argue that the coefficients for the political costs of extracting resources reflect undue constraint on the variance in GNP within each of the three groups more than they express the effect of our political variable itself. To see if this was indeed true, we allowed per capita GNP to vary within each level of economic development. The regressions obtained are shown in table 8.

Table 8
The Full Model for Death Rates: Effect of per Capita GNP and Political Capacity as Expressed by Political Costs for Each Level of Economic Development
(Y = Death Rates, x = Political Costs, z = GNP per Capita)

Underdeveloped: $Y = 19 + .42x - .01z$
Developing: $Y = 12 + .37x - .00z$
Developed: $Y = 11 + .04x - .00z$
$N = 1,868$
$R^2 = .72$ (for GNP alone, $R^2 = .65$)

The least-squares estimates shown in table 8 clearly indicate that, even if we allow per capita product to vary within levels of development, we obtain results similar to those found in table 7. Thus our hypothesis seems to hold true even when per capita GNP is allowed to vary within levels of development. The results concerning the relation between political costs, economic development, and death rates can be clearly seen in the three-dimensional figure below (fig. 10).

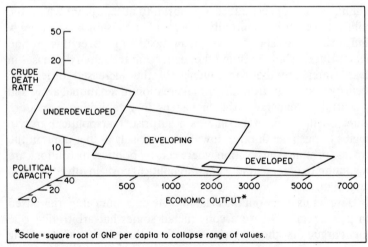

*Scale = square root of GNP per capita to collapse range of values.

Fig. 10.   Relation of mortality to political costs and wealth, 1950–75.

As we have already noted in our analysis of the effect of politics on fertility, the coefficient of determination for the general model is an "average" of the coefficients of determination derived for the separate regressions for each of the levels of economic development. The differences between the R^2s obtained by regressing fertility on both per capita GNP and political costs and those obtained by regressing it on GNP alone show that the measure of political costs adds a considerable amount to the variance in mortality explained by per capita GNP (see table 9).

Table 9
Regression of Death Rates on per Capita GNP and Political Capacity as Expressed by Political Costs for Each Level of Development

	Coefficients Underdeveloped ($N = 726$)	Coefficients Developing ($N = 729$)	Coefficients Developed ($N = 413$)
Per capita GNP	.01	.00	.00
Political costs	.42	.37	.04
R_1^2	.26	.18	.46
Per capita GNP alone	.01	.00	.00
R_2^2	.08	.05	.43
$R_1^2 - R_2^2$	.18	.13	.03

Again, within each group politics contributes a larger proportion than economics to variance explained in the underdeveloped and developing groups.

Finally, when we concentrate on the nondeveloped world and replicate the model set forth in table 6, our expectations are again confirmed (see table 10).

Table 10
Effects of GNP/Population and Political Costs on Death Rates of Underdeveloped and Developing Nations
(Y = Death Rates, x = Political Costs, z = GNP/Population)

Underdeveloped: $Y = 20 + .42x - .01z$
Developing: $Y = 12 + .37x + .00z$
$R^2 = .50$ (R^2 for GNP/Population alone $= .40$)
$N = 1,455$

The effects of political change on mortality are clearly less pronounced than those of economic development.

Conclusion

Let us briefly review our findings. The analysis confirms our hypotheses. Judging by our results, there can be no question that, as we suspected, growth in political capacity is indeed a determinant of the movement of fertility and mortality rates during development. Political growth under conditions of development affects vital rates in the same manner as economic and social development itself is known to do, pushing both fertility and mortality down to the low levels enjoyed by developed countries. The movement of the measures of the marginal political costs involved in extracting resources and the movement of the measures of vital rates are positively related, though the strength of the relation varies across levels of economic development. The overall results obtained for the entire sample of countries are quite clear: politics plays a significant role in determining patterns of demographic behavior among national populations.

All the effects appear most clearly when we disaggregate the sample of countries. It is in the nondeveloped world, as one would expect, that the most action is to be found regarding vital rates. So far as decreases in fertility are concerned, when we take underdeveloped and developing countries together and regress fertility on both economic and political development, growth in political capacity emerges as a potent factor in sending birthrates down. In short, a much larger share of the variance in birthrates is explained. And when we advance further and explore the link between political costs, increments in income, and fertility at each level of economic development, we find, as we suspected, that in underdeveloped countries the downward movement in vital rates brought about by growth in the political system is feeble because the political system is still weak and its expansion is slow and costly. Moreover, the decline is blunted at this point because the slight increase in income and the corresponding minor improvement in economic conditions have the effect of pushing birthrates up. The economic and political influences do not, however, entirely cancel each other out; the effects of political expansion are still significant. Even weak impulses emanating from the slowly and painfully expanding political system achieve substantial reductions because, in the underdeveloped world, birthrates are very high and one can therefore bring about a pronounced decrease with little effort.

It is at the developing level that major decreases in fertility rates occur. This accelerated decline in birthrates results from the combination of a rapidly expanding political system made possible by lower marginal costs and a rapidly increasing fund of economic resources. It is during this developing stage that most of the change in fertility rates takes place. With respect to fertility the poorest nations in this group still display the behavior patterns of underdeveloped countries, while the richest have managed in some cases to bring their birthrates to a point lower than those observed in the least advanced of the OECD countries. At this level of development both socioeconomic development and political capacity push toward reduction and result in major decreases in fertility.

In the developed group, finally, political change does not have much influence at all on birthrates, failing to reduce fertility *even further* than it has been already. As we have repeatedly stated, this is due to the fact that fertility rates are already very low and political expansion, if it exists at all, has again become very slow and very costly.

The findings regarding the link between mortality and political costs reveal that, for our entire sample of nations, political change has important effects, bringing mortality to the low levels that make the developed world the envy of less fortunate, nondeveloped populations. Yet the relation here is different from the one we found for fertility. As before, it is in the nondeveloped world that we discover the strongest connection. But if we separate the nondeveloped from the developed world and examine the relation between politico-economic change and mortality only in the former, we find that political change does indeed play a significant role in bringing mortality down but that socioeconomic change plays, in this instance, an even more important part. But it is when we pass on to examine the role of political and socioeconomic change within each group individually that we really see what is going on. In the underdeveloped group, political development clearly assumes dominance, explaining four-fifths of all the variance that can be explained. In the developing group, political development accounts for some two-thirds of the variance explained. In the OECD countries, finally, political change explains very little of the change in death rates.

One last point. If our analysis is correct, and if we do indeed find at work in the world the politico-demographic transition we have described here, it is clear that the real culprit in the population explosion that has shattered the structures of the international system in recent decades is political development. It is because of political development that the millennial balance between births and deaths has come unstuck. And, most important, it will be the continuing expansion of political systems, though aided in many decisive ways by economic growth and social change, that may at length bring fertility and mortality back into balance.

5 Conclusion

We shall try at this point to weave together all the threads spun out through the pages of this slim volume. After some introductory remarks, we shall review the nub of our discussion regarding the demographic transition, regarding the relation between the political and demographic transitions, regarding each of the variables studied in our experiment, and particularly regarding the measure of political capacity furnished by the estimation of the costs involved in extracting the resources required for the running and expansion of the state. We shall then turn to the principal results of our analysis. We shall avoid going into detail, focusing only on the main points made in the preceding pages. Then in an epilogue we shall examine the possible implications of the connections we have established between political development and vital rates.

We cannot hope to resist entirely feeling some elation, even though it is obvious that the results presented here are tentative at best and even though, clearly, what we have discovered needs to be validated again by replicating our tests using better data and more sophisticated methods. Nevertheless, we have identified a connection between the expansion of governmental power under conditions of development and change in vital rates. But other connections may exist. In any event, the massive transformation the political system undergoes during the process of development now stands revealed as a determinant of the evolution of vital rates. And much more important to those interested in political change rather than demographic behavior, this book presents a new way of measuring political development.

Here we should remind the reader of a suggestion we made in the Introduction. What we have attempted here can be viewed from three different angles of vision, for three groups of readers may find our ideas of interest: scholars specializing in demography, scholars interested in the behavior of political systems, and researchers interested in development as a whole.

We hope that all three groups will find something of value in everything we have had to say. Demographers, however, are likely to be most interested in our attempt to explain changes in vital rates among national populations more completely than present demographic theory can do. To them our work on measuring the capacity of political systems will be little more than an exercise in index construction and therefore of secondary importance.

Our colleagues in the field of politics are more likely to view this index construction as the main event. The effort to explore the demographic effects of political development as measured by our new model will accordingly represent to them simply an attempt to see whether the measure really works. From this second point of view, the phenomenon to be explained is less important than the validation of the measure. For if the new measure proposed here does in fact work, it will permit political scientists to monitor the behavior of whole political systems in a systematic and rigorous fashion, thus enabling them to undertake comparisons not possible up to now, beyond the mere "eyeballing" of the data.

As we noted at the beginning of this book, both of these angles of vision are entirely legitimate, and the reader may freely choose either one. But to a third subset of readers neither approach will by itself prove sufficient. To these scholars, the interest will lie in the elaboration of a code enabling one to define and analyze more precisely than before the many different political, demographic, and socioeconomic changes at the root of national development at large. We hope, then, that they will find both sides of our experiment here equally intriguing. We shall comment further on this point below when we come to what we ourselves consider a most important, and indeed exciting, moment in any new research enterprise: the construction of agendas for future research.

We have offered what we believe is a more advanced diagnosis of the interaction between the political and demographic transitions. One is tempted, however, to think beyond simple diagnosis. The asymmetries of economic, demographic, and political development we have discussed in this work create massive dislocation in the lives of hundreds of millions of people. Such problems demand solutions. What, if anything, can be done? And, more to the point, what can be done by government? Any such questions clearly go beyond our data. We will nevertheless conclude, in the Epilogue, by considering the possible openings for social engineering that our discussion reveals.

The Demographic Transition

There are only a few theories in the social sciences that offer an overview of any very broad terrain. The demographic transition theory is one of these. At the time of the theory's conception, many invoked the importance of interdisciplinary approaches to the problem of development. But of the responses to such calls, very few showed how much could be understood if one approached macrosocial phenomena using empirical data as well as an interdisciplinary perspective. The theory of the demographic transition has permitted the systematic application of serious thought to the large-scale structural changes that make up what is commonly referred to as "national development." Specifically, it has pointed to the way the economic, social, and demographic changes underpinning the massive transformation of socioeconomic, demographic, and political systems came together.

At the core of the theory of the demographic transition, we found the proposition that large-scale structural, economic, and social change was responsible for the decrease in birth and death rates in national populations. Death rates decreased before birthrates, creating a rapid increase in the population and sharp changes in the age structure of the nation. It was also clearly implied that these changes, once they had occurred, were, with minor and temporary fluctuations in their line of progress, irreversible—barring, of course, worldwide catastrophes. It was also implied that the changes in demographic behavior undergone by Western European nations would eventually be repeated by the developing and the underdeveloped portions of the world as well.

Some of these expectations, however, were not borne out by events in the immediate post-World War II period. In the midst of an era of unparalleled, almost universal, economic prosperity, birthrates suddenly reached new highs and death rates dropped further than expected owing to advances in the medical sciences. The population of the developed world grew at a very fast clip. Especially in North America, the fifties and sixties became the age of the child. The young adults of this new era seemed to rearrange the basic patterns of Western life. Abandoning the cities, they moved to more spacious surroundings in the suburbs and settled down with great seriousness to the task of having and rearing children. The fear of imminent population decline was replaced by fear of an uncontrolled population boom. Worse still, in the developing world a veritable population explosion accompanied the plunging death rates. Alarm spread, and the cry went out to bring fertility down. Governments and experts combined their efforts in founding programs aimed at population control. But in the seventies things again took a new turn. Under the apparent impetus of a return to hard economic times, birthrates once again plunged throughout the developed world, and the rates of growth in the developing world began to decelerate. It started to look as if the expectations of the demographic transition theory were finally coming true.

Regardless of other criticisms, the view that high birth and death rates become low birth and death rates solely as a result of socioeconomic development is seriously lacking in that it overlooks the effect on vital rates of political or state expansion (or political development). In other words, our criticism of previous explanations is that they did not see the transition in the political system as a factor in the transition of the demographic system. We should emphasize that our view and the findings we present do not contradict other attempts to account for the variation in demographic behavior; they complement them.

The Independent Variables

Political Change

There was, however, good reason for not taking into account the impact of politics on vital rates: there was simply no way of determining, in any systematic or rigorous fashion, what the political changes in question really were, and there was therefore no way of measuring their effects. The responsibility for this must be laid at the door of students of political institutions and behavior.

But now, at last, a measure of political development has become available. The measure in question has two points of reference: one is the actual performance of a given government in raising revenue; the other is the estimate of what a given government could be expected to raise in revenue if the political system operated at its very best. The measure we propose is related to the difference between the two. And the reason this difference —which estimates political costs—can serve as an indicator of political capacity is that the link between the two has been specified, at least in general terms.

Several points should be kept in mind. First, why measure the shortfall? Why not, rather, measure the system's actual performance, what it actually succeeds in extracting in the way of revenues? Unfortunately, no simpler, more direct method will work. The measure used to index the extractive capacity of the political system is the amount of taxes the system has collected as a share of GNP. But this sum is the product of both political and economic factors. It is enormously difficult to separate the contributions of politics and the economy in the total result. And yet this separation is essential to our purposes. One must go the extra, tortuous mile. As the reader will recall, it was in answer to this need that we devised the measure of political costs. This measure was almost free of the sort of ambiguity that arises from confusion of economic and political factors. In essence, we constructed it by estimating the very maximum a political system could possibly extract in taxes, taking the actual amount collected as an obvious indicator of extractive performance, and interpreting the difference between the two as a measurement of what the political system has to give up to gather in those resources it does in fact manage to acquire.

The maximum share that systems could possibly extract was determined by observing the tax behavior of countries locked in mortal military combat. We believed such countries would try as hard as they could to get the needed resources because their very existence would be at stake. The performance of the country that did best in this regard could then stand as the standard for all other nations at roughly the same level of economic development. The performance of North Vietnam in the Vietnam War, extracting 47 percent of the national gross product, and the performance of Great Britain in World War II, allocating 54 percent of national resources to defense, were used as the standards for developing and developed countries respectively. The index of the maximum was adjusted to take into account economic differences in the tax bases of the countries in the sample. The measure of resources actually collected was adjusted by taking policy preferences into account.

The difference between the maximum revenues a country can be expected to extract and what it actually succeeds in collecting was viewed as a measure of political costs. The reasons for this may be briefly restated as follows. All governments need or at least want all the resources they can get. If they fail to extract all they possibly can, it is because they cannot pay the political price of expanding their revenues—the "interest" required to buy the support of the various factions, rebel parties, and pressure groups with which they have to deal in order to govern.

What is the price in question? There are two sets of costs involved. One set arises from the need to expand the fund of available resources so as to build up and maintain the bureaucracies necessary to extract resources regularly and continuously or to extract even greater amounts of resources as required. The other set of costs is the expenditure incurred to suppress resistance to the will of the central authority, notably as regards its demands for more resources. That resistance is itself of two types. Initially, it is rooted in nationalistic or separatist ethnic, linguistic, religious, or simply territorial hostility toward the rising central power on the part of marginal groups seeking to preserve their autonomy against the state's attempts to expand its rule. This was, for instance, the historical experience of Europe at the beginning of the developmental process and is the experience of developing countries today. Once a country has begun to develop, however, the social and economic process spawns new forms of resistance from groups that development itself brings into existence. As governments grow ever more dependent for resources on the performance of their economic systems, the new economic elites soon find representation in the coalitions that rule the nation and enjoy the support of vast clienteles. Their power comes increasingly to bear, exerting considerable influence over government decisions on how much of the general pool of resources the state will absorb for its own uses and how the remainder will be spent. But whatever form of resistance they encounter, the reason countries fail to extract anywhere near the maximum possible is that they do not have the resources to pay the costs involved in expanding the levels of extraction they have already reached. They are, indeed, caught in a vicious circle in that the failure to extract the necessary resources in turn makes it difficult, if not impossible, to pay for the bureaucracies and the repressive mechanisms needed to compel consent to their demands. To *raise* more resources, they *need* more resources, but these are precisely the resources they find themselves unable to get.

Political costs are related to capacity in a very specific way. Costs are high when nations are at either extreme of the developmental continuum (i.e., when they are still wholly undeveloped or are already developed), but costs are low when nations are actively engaged in the process of development itself. Thus, for the nondeveloped world as a whole the relation between costs and capacity is inverse while in developed countries, though costs rise once more, capacity stabilizes at a high level, and we assume that, eventually, costs do as well. In any event, it is the clearly inverse relation between costs and capacity that permits us to use political costs as an *indicator* of capacity. And using political costs as a measure of political capacity—albeit a rather roundabout way of obtaining an indicator of political development—in turn provides us with an indicator of political performance we know to be largely uncontaminated by economic influences.

Socioeconomic Factors

It was clear, of course, that political growth is not the only "cause" of decrease in vital rates and that other, strictly psychosocial and economic factors play a critical role in this connection. We therefore had to incorporate in our model some index of these other factors. We decided, however, not to use a large number of socioeconomic indicators, choosing to summarize them all collectively by using per capita GNP alone. The reason for our choice was that per capita product is found to reflect the effects of other factors that were not being measured directly. Equally important was the fact that the effects of the political measure were not correlated to any appreciable extent with the other socioeconomic variables represented by per capita GNP.

The Dependent Variables: Vital Rates

Compared with the difficulties we encountered in trying to index the "causes" of the decline in vital rates, data for our dependent variables were fairly easy to come by. We used crude rates of births and deaths as our dependent variables. Even here, however, adjustments were necessary. We had to adjust for age structures, since, left unadjusted, crude rates would significantly distort any cross-national comparisons. The mortality rate of a rapidly growing population, for example, may easily be underestimated if in the national population includes a large number of very young people. We noted in this respect that, without adjustment, the death rates of Greece or Spain would appear lower than those of Germany, even though there can be no question that Germany enjoys a higher level of economic development than either Greece or Spain. Similarly, crude birthrates may lead to an overestimation of fertility if the national population contains a large number of young people. The age-specific data we needed were not equally available for all the countries in our sample, and we had to use different procedures in making the required adjustments for developed and developing countries.

The Analysis

What did we think we would find, and what did we in fact find?

First, a comment. There inevitably were problems owing to missing data. Quite important was the regrettable omission from the sample of a number of countries whose political capacity could not be estimated. The model we used grouped the countries in our sample according to per capita product into underdeveloped, developing, and developed nations. This is what is usually done when one wishes to compare countries at sharply different levels of development. The grouping permitted us to control substantially for the effects that economic development may have had on the dependent variables while still allowing for considerable variation in vital rates within each group. This in turn allowed some linear·

analysis of the effects of political change on vital rates within each group and for the international system as a whole.

Now to the results. Our findings bore out our expectations. First, the curvilinear trajectory we expected for political costs, moving from high to low and then to high again, was exactly what we discovered. The curve was not as smooth as we expected because, as we indicated a moment ago, a number of countries were omitted from our sample. In the present era there are no countries still at the very first stage of building a state structure, and as a result political costs as measured for the underdeveloped group in our sample were lower than they would otherwise have been—lower, to be precise, than the highs posted by the developed countries. We found, moreover, a sharp rise in the structure of political costs between the developing and the developed countries in our sample. We again speculate that the sharpness of the rise reflects the fact that a number of communist countries halfway between the developing and the developed world are missing from our sample—omitted because there is no way to estimate the political capacity of communist countries—and the fact that the tiny group of countries at this level of development that we did include were lumped either with the developing or the developed groups. There were not enough of them to enable us to do anything else. Had it been possible to avoid both these sources of distortion, the curve would have been smooth and symmetrical.

For the effect of political growth on vital rates, our findings were very much in keeping with our expectations. Regarding fertility, in the underdeveloped countries politics had a considerable effect on birthrates. But it was in the developing countries —nations where a state structure is already in place, political capacity is much higher, political costs are much lower, and the possibilities for expansion are therefore much stronger—that politics was found to account for the largest portion of the observed variance in rates of birth. This is precisely as we expected. And in the OECD countries, as we expected, the data showed that the effects of politics on birthrates are at best extremely weak.

The story with respect to death rates is as follows. The strongest impact of political growth on death rates is found in underdeveloped countries. In developing countries, the effect is strong, but much weaker than in the underdeveloped group; and in the developed world, as with birthrates, political factors explain very little of the very small movement observed in death rates. Superficially, it seems contradictory that political factors should have such a very strong effect precisely at that stage in the overall process of development when we argue that the capacity of the political system is at its lowest and the costs of expansion and development are at their highest. But, on reflection, this is not really the case. Building up the institutions that form the core of the state structure—the military, paramilitary and civil bureaucracies—is an objective the state structure must attain in order to survive and grow. Cost what it may, a state must have an army, a police force, and a civil bureaucracy in order to reach the population, impose its rule, and extract resources. At this point in the growth of the state, the feeling is let cost be damned. But the existence and activity of these institutions are precisely what generate the conditions of relative order, security, and peace conducive to at least an initial reduction in death rates. There are, moreover, countless illustrations among the emergent nations of the contemporary era in which the state has provided itself with a large military force and equipped it with spanking new military equipment long before doing anything else in the nation, but in which, despite the absence of health, sanitation, education, and other crucial government programs, mortality has nevertheless decreased.

Let us return to the main question examined in this book and make, at last, some concluding comments. We shall come back to an observation made at the very end of the chapter containing our analysis. Our findings regarding the relation between vital rates and political change are clearly in line with what we expected, but they are nevertheless to some extent perplexing. If death rates plunge under the influence of political change, then clearly the population explosion is a result of early political development, particularly in those cases where the growth of the state not only has introduced a degree of law and order into the system but, also very important, has brought with it modern medical and sanitary practices ingested by the system from the outside as well as economic activity stimulated in a variety of ways by external sources. Our findings suggest that, in the initial period of national development, political development is the culprit responsible for the scissors movement between births and deaths. But, as our analysis shows, if political development continues at a strong pace, then the growth of central political power is in fact the first and perhaps the major source of stimuli leading to the eventual reduction of fertility rates. Low levels of political development trigger demographic growth by lowering death rates; but high levels of state growth help mightily in providing their own corrective, closing the two blades of the scissors once more by exerting pressure that tends to lower fertility rates and return the system to stability. In cases where political development passes over into political decay, as some have alleged does eventually happen, there is little hope for the countries affected. We should state that we have looked into this matter and found evidence that, in fact, "political development" continues everywhere. One is once again impressed by the profound wisdom contained in the opening lines of Samuel Huntington's *Political Order in Changing Societies*: "The most important political distinction among countries concerns not their form of government but their degree of government."[1]

Yes, the capacity of government makes a difference. A new determinant of demographic behavior has been found.

Epilogue: Beyond the Data

We have not finished; not quite. It is not yet time for the reader to rise with a sigh and shut the book. The questions we wish to raise now lie a considerable distance beyond our data. Here our thoughts turn toward the first formulation of an entirely new set of propositions and how, perhaps, they might be tested. Admittedly, these speculations are as yet only vague intuitions struggling to come forth in the form of crisp hypotheses. Still, however shadowy for the moment, these speculations have a logical place in this book. It is, besides, always right to end one work by suggesting the beginning of another.

There are two sets of ideas we wish to present. One deals with some thoughts on what can be done, the other with the relevance of our politico-demographic findings.

What Can Be Done?

In the preceding pages we have talked solely about the reasons for the changes in vital rates and the resulting age structures that accompany the socioeconomic development of national societies. We hope we have demonstrated to our readers' satisfaction that one more factor than previously recognized is responsible for the large-scale demographic changes that have characterized development both historically and in present-day experience. As we found, the transformation of the demographic system under conditions of development is brought about not only by massive changes in productivity and social structures, but also by the massive changes that take place in the developing and expanding political system. The state of political development, as the reader is by now well aware, was found to be a major direct reason for the enormous increases and decreases in the fertility of national populations. Political development, moreover, triggered the sharp changes in mortality rates that resulted in the population explosion in the post-World War II era. Of those who applauded the incredible achievement of the postwar American international order in permitting decolonization and the establishment of firmer indigenous authorities in the new nations that came into being in the fifties and sixties, few foresaw that one consequence of this achievement would be a floodtide of births, with no balancing rise in death rates, that would threaten for a time to erode any chance of development in the new nations and to undermine the stability of the entire international system. On the other hand, political change was also found to play a major role in fostering the long-hoped-for deceleration in fertility of which signs have recently appeared in the developing world, a deceleration that seems to have occurred largely, though by no means entirely, in the absence of the massive socioeconomic changes that have heretofore been thought essential for declines in vital rates.

Politics and the growth of central government power have, then, for the first time been shown to be determinants of demographic trends. This being the case, it seems an appropriate moment to ask new questions, questions it has not been possible to ask before.

Thus far we have discussed only diagnoses. Scholars are readily suspected, not without reason, of professional bias against the Marxian dictum that the world needs not to be understood, but to be changed. The view that change is needed is often, and rightly, the prevailing one; the world is sick to death of diagnoses. Yet in this book we have not once turned to the question of remedies, of what can actually be done to stem or at least control the oncoming and receding human tides discernible in changes in vital rates. But not only does this question give access to important areas of new knowledge hitherto closed to us; it is also, at the same time, of immense practical importance. For the massive fluctuations in vital rates with which we have been dealing create vast social, economic, and political dislocations and upheavals and cause untold human misery. Can anything useful be done? More to the point, can anything useful be done by governments? Given our position that the extent of political development influences vital rates irrespective of the particular policies governments may adopt in demographic matters, can it be that birth control programs in the less developed world are like so many other human activities —undertaken because they relieve the anxieties of the actors, yet with no real effect on the problems they are meant to solve?

The expansion of central government power and its effects on demographic behavior do not in themselves constitute an answer to the questions we are posing. One cannot infer from the discovery of the profound but entirely *unintended* demographic consequences of the growth of government that government also has the capacity to influence birthrates *intentionally* either by changing their course or by attempting to reinforce the trend observed in fertility before government decided to intervene. It would be ironic if it were finally to be established that, though the expansion of government power has profound unintended demographic consequences, governments are nevertheless powerless when it comes to implementing deliberate policies aimed at redirecting the demographic trends their own rise has set in motion.[1] We know the expansion of government power is non-manipulable, at least in the short run, in much the same way that socioeconomic structures, the other fundamental determinants of fertility and mortality, resist direct manipulation. But, of course, government allocations of resources *are* manipulable. The key question is, Do these programs make any difference, and if so, precisely how much of a difference?

There are really two very broad questions at issue here, each of which ought to be considered separately.

The first question is as follows: Can governments make fertility rates move faster in the direction in which they are already moving? In more practical terms, Can the government of a country in which fertility is already declining as part of the complex of unintended changes in the economic, social, and political structures of society consequent upon development measurably increase the rate of such reduction by instituting policies to induce people to reduce the size of their families?

The second question goes like this: Can governmental power be used to increase fertility once it has dropped to the low levels

prevalent in developed countries where urbanization, industrialization, education, greater freedom of choice for women, and
similar factors have brought fertility to hover just above, at, or
even below replacement levels? Can governmental power be used
in this fashion?

Obtaining answers to these questions is, as any expert in the
field well knows, an enormously complicated business. We believe, however, that our new finding connecting political change
and change in vital rates is relevant to these questions, and we
should like to state how this is so. Moreover, exploring the effects
of the growth of the political system on fertility is an exquisite test
of the limits of government power. It enables us to probe the
extent to which governments can redirect human behavior against
the wishes of their subjects in a matter where their subjects'
cooperation is essential.

The importance of such a test and of the inferences that can be
based on its results cannot be overemphasized. These are tests of
the level of government development and of government capacity
to govern. We have already indicated why we think this is so. All
governments are charged with two fundamental tasks: to provide
for the common defense against external threat, and to manage the
working of society in such a way as to ensure as far as possible that
resources and demands for resources remain roughly in balance. A
major factor in regulating demand is regulating the number of
people in the polity. If it can be demonstrated that our measure of
the degree of development achieved by a political system is clearly
connected to the government's performance in deliberate attempts
to influence the reproductive behavior of individual couples in
meeting collective needs, then one can have very little doubt of
that government's ascendancy over its people. For, clearly, if
government can induce its subjects, in the name of the collectivity,
to refrain from doing what they believe is in their own interest,
then one has the best test of governmental power one could
imagine. Such a test would validate once again, even more
convincingly, the measures of political capacity we have devised.
And the business of comparing political systems by component or
in their totality will proceed more fruitfully if we can be assured of
the validity of the measures used in such comparisons. But let us
repeat: there are no answers yet to the questions posed here. What

follows are only rough and tentative hypotheses to be explored in subsequent research and ideas about the approaches future researchers might use in exploring them.

Now back to the first question. Are family-planning programs worthwhile? There are strong advocates of such programs, but there are also serious doubters posing serious doubts. Are the pleas that such programs be continued and strengthened due not to the fact that they can genuinely make enough of a difference, but rather to a sense that, effective or not, they are all that *can* be done? How much of a difference does a family-planning program actually make? Does it make any difference at all?

There are two ways to view this question. One concern is the quality of life enjoyed by the recipients of family-planning services: concern over the physical and mental health of mother and father, over the dilution of family resources, over the life chances of children and parents, all affected by the appearance of unwanted progeny. These are clearly issues of individual needs—human needs—matters of the quality of life of individuals. The second set of concerns is more national in character, rooted in the relation between high rates of national fertility, low productivity, and economic development. These two sets of problems are obviously to some extent interconnected, but they are also largely independent of each other. One might be tempted to view the first set as the preoccupations of the mass publics themselves and the second as representing the preoccupations of their leaders.

This second set of questions represents our chief and, indeed, our sole concern here. Freedman and Berelson have summarized in superb fashion the doubts and the evidence in regarding family-planning programs from this national point of view:

—that whatever family planning can contribute to fertility decline is insufficient to the need
—that observed declines in the presence of family planning efforts would have occurred anyway, in a trivially longer time
—that family planning can perhaps accelerate an existing decline, slightly, but cannot initiate one in a traditional society
—that family planning can "work" only in relatively advantaged societies, where it is less needed
—that family planning can "work" only among the relatively

better-off sectors of a developing population, who would soon come to it anyway, but not among the uneducated rural masses that make up such countries
—that family planning programs can perhaps "skim the cream" of available motivation in such societies but cannot generate motivation and hence have no staying power
—that expressions of interest in family planning found in fertility surveys are not valid indicators of subsequent behavior
—that current norms as to family size leave little room for family planning interventions toward fertility decline
—that family planning interest, such as it is, is found too late in the reproductive career to make much difference from a demographic standpoint
—that for the various reasons above a new contraceptive technology will not make much difference either
—that only a massive social and economic transformation and the attendant structural changes can bring about the necessary decline, in the absence of state impositions.[2]

The doubts expressed in the criticisms cited above are forceful and clear, and Freedman and Berelson supply as many answers as they can, but no *definitive* answers can in fact be given. Attempts to decide the matter one way or the other are enormously difficult, for this involves disentangling the social, economic, and psychological influences—influences to which we have now added the political effects—from the behavior strictly affected by population limitation programs themselves. Such attempts are plagued with problems of method, concept, and data. The best one can say is that the services provided by family-planning programs certainly make a difference at the individual level. To the extent that some portion of the population has been persuaded to use birth control, which they would otherwise not have done or would have postponed doing, to that extent such programs will have enhanced the well-being of all members of the family. There seems to be substantial evidence that the cumulative effect of such individual changes in behavior is by no means insignificant and that many of the doubts about the identity of the acceptors are not in fact correct. But the question at issue here is whether family planning makes *enough* of a difference at the *collective* level to offer a real answer to the problem of high fertility, and from this point of view the answer certainly cannot be an unqualified yes. No definitive answer can be given, and doubts will remain.

There is no doubt, however, that population programs can perform better than they do at present; more precisely, there is no question that the resources expended on efforts to control fertility could be spent more effectively, and perhaps much more efficiently, than they are now. In a way, we are asking, What are the constituents of a successful population program? It is clear that the determinants of successful population programs are the same as the determinants of declines in fertility. And it is at this point that all we have written in the preceding pages might be of importance.

It has been customary to look at three factors in evaluating population programs: social conditions, economic conditions, and the administration of the program itself. Political commitment has also been judged important. But political commitment has often been conceived as the strong personal preferences of the relevant political or administrative leaders: a health minister, a prime minister, a party leader. But this definition of political commitment completely misses the mark.

The case of China will drive the point home. The *social*, *economic*, and *demographic* setting for fertility control in China is poor, but "political commitment" has been high and the results have been nothing short of astounding. It is precisely at this point, however, that, in light of what we have seen in this book, the concept of "political commitment" has to be redefined. The reader will recognize our constant refrain. Political action is not the result of the "will" or "commitment" of political leaders, that is, of strongly held preferences on the part of ruling elites. The degree of political action will occur in proportion to the degree of political organization and capacity. And the degree of the political capacity to act in turn depends first on the structure of the coalitions of elites who direct action from the top of the political pyramid and, second, on the adequacy of the mechanisms of extraction, penetration, and repression that make up the governmental system. Viewed in this perspective, indeed, the degree of effective political action is finally a function of the strength of the opposition to a particular action. The reader will recognize the argument. The price of establishing and maintaining the organization and the price of overcoming opposition to government authority are what we have defined as the "political costs" of government. If the argument in this book is in any way valid, the reason the Chinese program has been so successful is not that Chinese leaders are more committed in a volitional sense; it is that the political costs of expanding the system, and thus of the government's capacity to impose its will, are very low, and coupled even with few resources and a very high rate of fertility this makes a powerful combination. This brings us to the last component of our equation: the amount of resources allocated to make the policy a reality.

In response, then, to the question of how specific conditions determine the success of population planning programs, we advance the hypothesis that social and economic factors may have been less significant than *the capacity of the political system* and that the combination of the amount of resources allocated and the degree of political capacity may really hold the key. But, clearly, political capacity is not manipulable, at least not in the short run. The government of a nation with a weak political system cannot choose whether or not to use the existing government structure. If the political system is weak, resources allocated to family planning, or any other program for that matter, will be used inefficiently, often with a great deal of waste—all of which has considerable implications for international aid. For while local governments may have no choice in the matter, international donors can in fact choose where to contribute resources. In any event, they should enter into eleemosynary activities with their eyes open: returns on their aid will be proportionate to the capacity of the recipient's political structure to reach its own population.

Let us turn to the question whether governments can turn fertility upward once development is high and fertility has moved to low levels. Here too there are no definitive answers. Governments have tried to stimulate birthrates in the past. In the 1930s European governments, frightened because birthrates had fallen so low as barely to reach replacement levels where there were not in fact declines in population, moved to raise fertility. Once embarked on this course, they used any means at their command: persuasion through education and propaganda and incentives in the form of family allowances, health care, subsidies for housing, free vacations for children, reduction in school fees, tax reductions, welfare legislation to improve the economic situation of large families, and the like. Some governments, that of the USSR, for example, sought to stimulate fertility by honoring motherhood and large families. Thus, the Soviet government awarded women with seven, eight, or nine children the Order of Motherhood Glory. Women with ten children were given the Order of Mother Heroine. And the effort was indeed heroic; parents everywhere would agree that such a title was fully earned and that, indeed, mothers and fathers of smaller families deserved such awards as well. Nor did governments confine themselves to offering incentives. States often used repressive measures. Abortion was declared a capital crime—Hitler, for one, ordered that it be punished by beheading—and modern methods of contraception were made illegal.

There is little evidence, however, that such measures were successful—that governments succeeded in convincing their people that the collective interests of the nation as a whole ought to take precedence over individual preferences for small families or that birthrates rose substantially. It may be that none of these government efforts lasted long enough. No sooner had European governments convinced themselves that they needed more people than they declared war on one another and started killing off the people they already had. Or perhaps the resources invested in the programs were simply insufficient. One cannot tell, and in fact this whole set of experiments has to date remained largely unexplored. Again, the problem of disentangling the influence of economic, political, social, and psychological forces from the effects of population programs is a difficult one, and there are many methodological, data, and conceptual obstacles standing in the way. Over the past few decades, moreover, the question whether governments can raise rates of fertility has not been a high priority either with governments themselves or with scholars; preoccupation has run the other way. It may now be coming back into favor, however, since population decline is reemerging in Europe. But as of now we do not know.

To say that no attention has been paid to government efforts at increasing fertility is not entirely true. At least one case has recently been the object of an excellent study: the efforts made by the government of Rumania to raise the rapidly falling birthrate of that country.[3] The Rumanian case has been used to illustrate the successful use of government power to alter fertility rates and the demographic posture of a national population. But it strikes us that this positive interpretation may be at least in part misleading, and we shall discuss the case very briefly to explain why.

The facts of the Rumanian case are these. The birthrate in Rumania was falling, as birthrates have been falling in other Eastern European and some Western European nations—in part as a result of socioeconomic development and, in the Eastern European nations, probably as a result of the harshness of life as well. By 1966 Rumanian birthrates had fallen to fourteen per thousand. Such a birthrate threatened to make the labor force insufficient to carry out the state's economic plan, so the government decided to intervene. The predominant method of birth control in Rumania had been abortion. Abortions had been provided free and were readily available through state facilities. Eighty percent of all conceptions were terminated in this way. In the face of the risk of crippling population decline, however, the government made abortion illegal and contraceptives difficult to obtain. A decree to this effect was issued in 1966. In the next year the birthrate shot up thirteen points, to twenty-seven per thousand. But since then the birthrate has been decreasing sharply, though it has remained somewhat higher than it would have been had the government not interfered, leaving Rumanians free to avail themselves of the abortion facilities the state had previously made available.

How is one to evaluate the Rumanian experience? Berelson compares the rise in birthrate achieved by the Rumanian authorities with the increases during the American baby boom after World War II and concludes that the Rumanian experience is evidence that government can do a great deal. He takes it, in short, as a sign of government power. We would argue the opposite. It depends, of course, on one's interests. Without doubt, the government's intervention substantially changed the country's demographic position. But if one is interested in government power and looks more closely at events in Rumania, it is equally undeniable that the government did not in fact convince Rumanians to change their fundamental behavior in regard to family size. Once they learned to circumvent the obstacles the government had thrown in their way, Rumanians pretty much returned to their previous patterns of behavior. We suspect that the Rumanian government may have achieved a one-time success that cannot be repeated or sustained. It does not therefore illustrate government power any more than windfall profits or winning a lottery provide evidence of entrepreneurial flair.

Berelson's Rumanian study is nevertheless enormously sugges-tive of what must be done to test the proposition that governments can increase fertility rates once they have bottomed out at the developed level. It has been said that the example of the attempts made by European governments in the thirties is not clear-cut enough because the investments made were not very great; the amount spent to support these efforts, though in some cases substantial, was not large enough to drive birthrates up again. But it does seem that some European nations are now beginning to make large investments in precisely the areas that will affect reproductive behavior. Will birthrates rise? Scholars interested in demography, in national development, and in testing govern-ment's capacity to govern, an issue that is all the rage just now, should not let the opportunity slip by.

On the Relevance of This Study

In the Introduction we raised two questions about the signifi-cance of the link between political growth and demographic behavior and about the relevance such a link, assuming one exists, may have to the peace and stability of the international system. The claim we made at that time requires brief adumbration here.

The connection between the political and demographic transi-tions may turn out to be a key to understanding how, and eventually even why, the transformation of the social environment we have come to call development occurs. We have said that modern development differs from developmental processes in premodern, preindustrial periods in that change in one sector of national life may attain sufficient magnitude and intensity to spark and help sustain change in other sectors. That changes in the social, economic, or political order of society are no longer contained, or even containable, within one sector is the key difference between development today and the feeble attempts at development in the past. It is our view that, to understand how modern development occurs, one must understand more about the links between the transformations arising in the different areas of political, economic, and social life: how the political and economic transitions are related, how these in turn are related to the transformation of the social structure, and so forth. If the findings of this book are confirmed by further research, then we hope we have put in place an important piece of the general puzzle of development. Till now it has been thought that only social and economic change could stimulate the demographic transformation associated with development. Now political change has been added to the list of determinants of the demographic transition. A new set of possible influences comes into view. Not only can political growth affect vital rates, but it can also encourage economic growth by bringing fertility down in underdeveloped countries afflicted with inordinately high birthrates. Our understanding of the mechanisms at work in the process we call development is certainly nowhere near the point where we can begin to describe what we think really happens when national development takes place. But we can describe much more than we could one or two decades ago. We hope this book contributes to that description.

The material presented here is relevant in yet another way. If the relation between political development and vital rates is what we have hypothesized it to be, then it is likely—though of course by no means certain—that countries today saddled with large populations and underdeveloped economies, but endowed with strong and effective political systems, should in fact have additional time—perhaps even enough time—to gather in at least a minimally sufficient reserve of human and material resources to let them develop economically. In a socioeconomic setting characterized by low economic productivity and high rates of fertility, a strong effective political system does double duty. First of all, it permits the collecting of needed resources from the widest possible subset of the productive population in the national society. This is essential if the people in the nation are very poor. Let us be clear. Low economic productivity and large population increases inevitably lead to progressive pauperization. Because individuals possess very little wealth, it is imperative that the central governmental authority be able to reach as many of its subjects as possible, to extract from each the tiny amount that can be spared and gather it in a central pool. To achieve this aim, political centralization, penetration, and perhaps even repression will prove essential.[4] But in the second place, and equally important, strong and effective political systems, owing to their intrusions, extractions, and ma-nipulations of people's lives, themselves reduce vital rates. This has been the subject of this book.

We have said that if the link proposed here is indeed found to exist, and we have found that it does, then the future should differ from current expectations not only for all the major underdevel-oped and developing countries in the world—India, China, Indo-nesia, Brazil, for example, and, somewhat behind them in size, Mexico and Nigeria—but for the rest of us as well. The implica-tions should be carefully pondered. The distribution of power in the world has undergone dramatic changes in the past hundred years, with the United States emerging as the uncontested first and the Soviet Union the unchallenged second most powerful nation in the world. The conditions behind the rise of these two powers to positions of preeminence are precisely the ones we have discussed: the timing, manner, point of departure, and speed of their demographic and political transition and industrialization.[5] One ought to bear in mind that the nearly constant national and international turmoil rife for almost a century now, the violent breaking up and reshaping of the geopolitical crust that provides the topography of international power, is intimately associated with the growth of the European colonial and industrial powers over the nineteenth century. The present political topography has emerged from the explosive growth of United States and Russian preeminence, and the rise of other potential major powers will transform the landscape yet again. Our findings suggest, then, that the present stability is very temporary and that in the decades ahead the distribution of power in the world is likely to change again. It is probable that China will emerge as a contender for power with the other two colossi. Whether China will in fact ascend to the position that could be hers given her political capacity and the size of her population will depend on whether she can develop economically—and it is of course not at all inevitable that China will succeed. The course she must follow will be arduous at best. But her chances of success are enhanced by her political control over the vast majority of her people, by her demonstrated ability to demand and receive immense sacrifices from them, and finally by the fact that the immense and crushing expansion of her state power has helped bring birthrates down to more or less manageable levels. We do not know whether it will happen, but we do know that it could not happen without the demographic transition brought about by her political development.

How ironic it all is. Who among us in the West, having decried China's turn to communism and lived through the painful political spasms it provoked over a decade, would have thought we would see the day when the amelioration of a frightening world problem, overpopulation, would be promoted by the political expansion made possible by the very shift to communism we all so passionately abhorred? Who would have thought the developmental mechanism would work in this way: that hope of bringing the population explosion under control would come not from a rise in economic productivity as everyone supposed (the underdeveloped world has not really improved its economic lot substantially) but from a rise of what is really political productivity? And who would have thought that an easing of the population problem today, by dramatically changing old distributions of power and demanding difficult adaptations to new circumstances, would be the harbinger of still a more difficult problem in the future? If, of course, such circumstances occur; and the ifs, as we noted earlier, are very real.

The battle for security, plenty, peace, and power will not be won with weapons. No careful accounting of the distribution of arms in the world today will give us a clue to our future security or to the future stability of the system. Nations will be made winners or losers by political, demographic, and economic change. Those countries that deal successfully with the problems discussed in this book will triumph over the others. If none succeed in dealing with such problems, then the status quo will not be preserved. All will lose.

Appendix 1: Regression Models

The model used to gauge the effects of political capacity on vital rates (see tables 3 and 7) is the following:

$$Y_i = \alpha + \sum_{j=1}^{2} \beta_j d_{ji} + \sum_{j=1}^{2} \gamma_j (d_{ji} x_i) + \delta x_i + \epsilon_i$$

where

Y_i = birthrates (or death rates)
x_i = scores of political capacity
d_{ji} = dummy variables for the categories of economic development:
  d_{1i} = 1 for an observation in the lowest category
      0 otherwise
  d_{2i} = 1 for an observation in the middle category
      0 otherwise.

The resulting regressions for each category of economic development are:

Underdeveloped: $Y_i = (\alpha + \beta_1) + (\gamma_1 + \delta)x_i + \epsilon_i$
Developing: $Y_i = (\alpha + \beta_2) + (\gamma_2 + \delta)x_i + \epsilon_i$
Developed: $Y_i = \alpha + \delta x_i + \epsilon_i$

The results presented in tables 3 and 7 are least-squares estimates of the coefficients above.

The model used to gauge the effects of political capacity on vital rates, allowing GNP per capita to vary within our categories of economic development (see tables 4 and 8), is the following:

$$Y_i = \alpha + \sum_{j=1}^{2} \beta_j d_{ji} + \sum_{j=1}^{2} \gamma_j (d_{ji} x_{1i}) + \sum_{j=1}^{2} \zeta_j (d_{ji} x_{2i}) + \sum_{j=1}^{2} \delta_j x_{ji} + \epsilon_i$$

where

Y_i = birth (or death) rates
x_{1i} = political capacity scores
x_{2i} = GNP per capita values
d_{ji} = dummy variables for the categories of economic development.

The resulting regressions for each category of economic development are:

Underdeveloped: $Y_i = (\alpha + \beta_1) + (\gamma_1 + \delta_1)x_{1i} + (\zeta_1 + \delta_2)x_{2i} + \epsilon_i$
Developing: $Y_i = (\alpha + \beta_2) + (\gamma_2 + \delta_1)x_{1i} + (\zeta_2 + \delta_2)x_{2i} + \epsilon_i$
Developed: $Y_i = \alpha + \delta_1 x_{1i} + \delta_2 x_{2i} + \epsilon_i$

The results presented in tables 4 and 8 are least-squares estimates of the coefficients above. All estimates, whether significant or not at the .05 level, were included in the results presented in all tables. However, even if we excluded the very few coefficients with $p < .05$, the results would be almost exactly the same.

Appendix 2: Data

Sample: Size and Composition

The sample used is not random because data for many developing nations are not available over time. The sample consisted of ninety nations; of these, forty-two had sufficient data for the entire period. Asterisks indicate OECD countries.

Algeria	1955, 1959-75
Angola	1955-74
*Australia	1953-75
*Austria	1953-75
*Belgium	1953-75
Bolivia	1955-75
Brazil	1953-75
Burundi	1960-75
Cameroon	1960-75
*Canada	1953-75
Central African Empire	1960-75
Chad	1960-75
Chile	1953-75
Colombia	1953-75
Congo	1960-75
Costa Rica	1955-75
*Denmark	1953-75
Dominican Republic	1953-75
Ecuador	1953-75
Egypt	1953-75
El Salvador	1953-75
Ethiopia	1956-75
*Finland	1953-75
133 Gabon	1960-75

Ghana	1955-75
Greece	1953-75
Guatemala	1953-75
Honduras	1953-75
India	1953-75
Iran	1953-75
Iraq	1953-75
*Ireland	1953-75
Israel	1953-75
*Italy	1953-75
Ivory Coast	1960-75
Jamaica	1953-75
*Japan	1953-75
Jordan	1960-75
Kenya	1953-75
Korea, Republic of	1955-75
Lesotho	1964-75
Liberia	1960-75
Libya	1963-75
Malagasy	1960-75
Malawi	1960-75
Malaysia	1955-75
Mauritania	1960-75
Mexico	1960-75
Morocco	1960-75
Mozambique	1960-75
Nepal	1960-75
*The Netherlands	1953-75
*New Zealand	1953-75
Nicaragua	1960-75
Nigeria	1953-75
*Norway	1953-75
Pakistan	1965-75
Panama	1953-75
Papua New Guinea	1961-75
Paraguay	1955-75
Peru	1953-75
Philippines	1953-75
Portugal	1953-75
Puerto Rico	1960, 1965, 1970-75

Rwanda	1960-75
Saudi Arabia	1960-75
Senegal	1963-74
Sierra Leone	1964-75
Somalia	1960-75
South Africa	1953-75
Spain	1955-75
Sri Lanka	1953-75
Sudan	1955-75
*Sweden	1953-75
Switzerland	1953-75
Syria	1955-75
Tanzania	1960-75
Thailand	1953-75
Togo	1960-75
Trinidad and Tobago	1953-75
Tunisia	1960-75
Turkey	1953-75
Uganda	1955-75
*United Kingdom	1953-75
*United States	1953-75
Upper Volta	1962-73
Uruguay	1953-75
Venezuela	1960-75
Zaire	1953-56, 1963-75
Zambia	1955-75

Data: Sources and Estimates

In collecting the components used in this study we relied on a variety of published and unpublished sources. Most were obtained from the World Bank, the International Monetary Fund, and the Agency for International Development, but some came from United States and other government sources and from individual monographs. In the following pages we describe each component with its sources and adjustments. A complete codebook will be made available through the Inter-university Consortium for Political and Social Research at the University of Michigan.

Demographic Variables

Population

Population figures for each year from 1950 through 1978 are taken from table 1.C—Annual Mid-Year Population by Region and Country or Area, 1950–2000, Medium Variant, in *World Population Trends and Prospects by Country, 1950–2000: Summary Report of the 1978 Assessment*, published by the United Nations. (Henceforth this report will be referred to as *Trends and Prospects, 1978*.)

Crude Rates

Crude birthrates and crude death rates come from table 2.B—Crude Birth and Death Rates, by Region and Country or Area, 1950–1975, in *Trends and Prospects, 1978*. The estimated crude rates are five-year averages for the intervals 1950–55, 1955–60, . . . , 1970–75. For our purposes these have been assigned to the years 1953, 1958, . . . , 1973. In countries where rates change rapidly during a given quinquennium, this arbitrary decision may introduce some bias. However, it is extremely unlikely that this bias affected the analysis in any significant way.

Age-Adjusted Crude Rates

Crude rates have been adjusted on two standard populations. The first adjustment uses the population of England and Wales specific for the year of the rate to be adjusted. That is, the population of England and Wales in 1955 is used as the standard for computing age-adjusted rates for the year 1955, the population in 1960 is used for the age-adjusted rates for 1960, and so on. The second adjustment uses the population of England and Wales in 1960 as the standard for all years. This approach eliminates whatever variation might be introduced by changing age structure in England and Wales and so is more appropriate for making comparisons over time.

Age-Adjusted Crude Death Rates

These have been computed differently for developed and for developing countries. For most developed countries, an age-adjusted crude death rate (CDR) was computed using direct standardization. Age-specific mortality rates (ASMRs) were collected for the years 1950, 1955, . . . , 1975 from various volumes of the *United Nations Demographic Yearbook*. The ASMRs were applied to the population of England and Wales as described above to obtain age-adjusted crude rates. For a few countries in certain years, ASMRs were unavailable. In these cases the age-adjusted CDRs were interpolated using estimated age-adjusted CDRs (computed in the same way as those for developing countries).

Direct standardization was not possible for developing countries, since for these nations the demographic yearbook data were both sporadic and of generally poor quality. Thus, for developing countries, age-specific mortality rates were estimated using life-table techniques. The estimated expectancy of life at birth was taken from table 3.B, Life Expectancy at Birth by Region and Country or Area, 1950–1975, in *Trends and Prospects, 1978*. These expectancies, like the crude rates, are five-year averages (1950–55, 1955–60, . . . , 1970–75) and are assigned to the years 1955, 1960, . . . , 1975. Using these life expectancies, we estimated ASMRs from the Western male family of the Coale-Demeny model life tables. The life-table ASMRs were then applied to the population of England and Wales, first for the specific year and then for 1960, to produce the two alternative age-adjusted crude death rates for the developing countries.

Use of this life-table technique assumes a stable population: that is, constant birth and death rates over a long period. This assumption is violated for many, perhaps most, developing countries. In some cases, for example countries that have experienced *rapid* declines in either mortality or fertility over the period studied, the bias introduced by the stable population models may be considerable. The extent to which this bias may affect the analysis cannot be known without further analysis.

Age-Adjusted Crude Birthrates

The crude birthrate (CBR) was adjusted using the proportion of women fifteen to forty-four in the total population as compared with a standard population. Again, two standards were used: the proportion of females fifteen to forty-four in England and Wales in the particular year for which the rate is computed, and the proportion of females fifteen to forty-four in England and Wales in 1960. Data on age structure by sex come from *Population by Sex and Age for Regions and Countries, 1950–2000, as Assessed in 1973: Medium Variant*, published by the United Nations. Data are available for 1950, 1955, . . . , 1975. The proportion of women fifteen to forty-four in the population was computed for each year and country. This proportion was then divided into the proportion of females fifteen to forty-four for England and Wales in the appropriate year or in 1960. The resulting quotient was then used to multiply the CBR to produce an age-adjusted CBR.

Total Output: Gross National Product and Gross Domestic Product

Two measures of gross product are used. Gross national product (GNP) is a measure of the total domestic and foreign output claimed by residents of a country. Gross domestic product (GDP) measures the total final output of a country including all goods produced and services rendered within its territory by residents and nonresidents, without regard to allocations among domestic and foreign claims. The difference between GNP and GDP is the net factor income from abroad.

For gross national product in constant 1976 United States dollars, 1,173 of the 1,455 nation-year data points for developing countries were taken from World Bank, *Socio-Economic Data Bank*, revised 29 January 1979. This is the source for virtually all years past 1959. Data from World Bank, *Socio-Economic Data Bank*, revised 13 October 1975, were converted to constant 1976 United States dollars for another 170 cases, almost entirely in the 1950s. Seventy data points were formed by making straight linear interpolations between extant data. Twenty-two data points were estimated or found in various miscellaneous sources.

For the 413 nation-years analyzed for developed nations, GNP in constant 1973/74 United States dollars was used. Eighty percent of the data were taken from World Bank, *Socio-Economic Data Bank*, revised 13 October 1975. The data for 1975 were taken from *OECD National Accounts, 1960–1977*, vol. 2, and were adjusted. The index used was based on variations in GDP using 1974 as the base year. Sixty-six data points, all in the 1950s, were taken from *OECD National Accounts, 1953–1969*, vol. 2, and were adjusted. The index used was based on variations in GDP using 1960 as the base year.

For developing nations, 95 percent of the data points for GDP were taken from World Bank, *Socio-Economic Data Bank*, revised 29 January 1979. Fifty-eight cases are linear interpolations of this data set. The remaining twenty-one data points are interpolated, extrapolated, or calculated on the basis of published and unpublished material.

For developed nations, 313 cases were taken from World Bank, *Socio-Economic Data Bank*, revised 13 October 1975. Ninety cases were taken from *OECD National Accounts, 1960–1977*, vol. 1. The remaining data points are taken from *OECD National Accounts, 1974*, vol. 2, *OECD Finland Economic Survey, 1976*, *OECD Netherlands Economic Survey, 1977*, and Krantz and Nilson, *Swedish National Product, 1961–1970*.

Mineral Production

Mineral production is defined as production from mining, quarrying, petroleum, and natural gases and is measured in local currency. For developing nations, the data are taken largely from World Bank, *Socio-Economic Data Bank*, revised 29 January 1979, and from World Bank, *Socio-Economic Data Bank*, revised 13 October 1975. These two data sets, with adjustments and linear interpolations, account for 87 percent of the data points for developing nations. A variety of other published and unpublished sources were used to fill out the data set, prominent among them being the *Yearbook of National Account Statistics* for various years.

The mining data for developed nations were taken mostly from the World Bank, *Socio-Economic Data Bank*, revised 13 October 1975, and *OECD National Accounts, 1960–1977*. The *United*

Nations Statistical Yearbooks of 1960, 1966, 1969, 1972, and 1975 also served as sources. The *Official Yearbook of the Commonwealth of Australia*, 1975 and 1976, completed the series for that nation; the *OECD National Accounts, 1974*, vol. 2, was used for Japan for the years 1965–69.

Tax

Tax data for the developing countries were needed for three variables: general government revenue, social security contributions, and nontax revenue.

General government revenue was taken largely from World Bank, *Socio-Economic Data Bank*, revised 29 January 1979. *United Nations Statistical Yearbooks* of 1957, 1962, 1965, 1969, and 1972 also supplied data points. For 162 nation-years, the relevant data could not be found. However, in 113 of these cases a figure representing or closely approximating our "adjusted tax" was found; the sources for these cases were many and varied but were generally national account statistics.

Social security tax figures were taken from World Bank, *Socio-Economic Data Bank*, revised 29 January 1979 and *United Nations Statistical Yearbooks*. In the vast majority of years, nations did not have social security programs, so that missing data could legitimately be replaced by zeros.

Data for nontax revenue were taken from World Bank, *Socio-Economic Data Bank*, revised 29 January 1979, *United Nations Statistical Yearbooks*, and the *Yearbook of National Account Statistics* for various years.

In fifty cases, the tax ratio (adjusted tax/GDP) had to be estimated. These cases were:

Algeria	1960, 1974
Brazil	1964-66
Burundi	1960-61, 1975
Cameroon	1960, 1975
Central African Empire	1960
Costa Rica	1955-59
Ethiopia	1956-60

Iran	1953
Libya	1965
Malawi	1960-62
Mozambique	1960
Niger	1974-75
Pakistan	1965, 1969
Rwanda	1960-62
Somalia	1960
Sri Lanka	1953-59
Sudan	1955-59, 1972
Uruguay	1974-75

For developed nations, most of the government revenue data were taken from World Bank, *Socio-Economic Data Bank*, revised 13 October 1975. *OECD National Accounts, 1960–1977* also supplied much of the data. Various OECD publications accounted for the remaining data points.

The World Bank, *Socio-Economic Data Bank*, revised 13 October 1975, was the source for a large part of the nontax revenue data for developed nations. *OECD National Accounts, 1960–1977* and *OECD Revenue Statistics, 1965–1978* also supplied many of the data points. A variety of *OECD National Accounts* and *OECD Revenue Statistics* were the source for the remaining data points.

For developed nations, data on social security revenue and social security expenditures were taken largely from World Bank, *Socio-Economic Data Bank*, revised 13 October 1975. *OECD National Accounts* for various years was also a prominent source, as was *OECD Revenue Statistics* for various years.

Notes

Introduction

1. R. Giffen, 1885 address to the Statistical Society of London. Reprinted in *Population and Development Review* 5, 2 (1979): 319–46; Nazli Choucri, "The Pervasiveness of Politics: Political Definitions of Population Issues," mimeographed (Hastings on Hudson, N.Y.: Institute of Society, Ethics, and the Life Sciences, December 1976); L. P. Wilkinson, "Classical Approaches to Population and Family Planning," *Population and Development Review* 4, 3 (September 1978): 439–55; G. D. Ness, "Politics and Population Growth," *Populi* 4, 3 (1977): 18–26.
2. For a first measure of this kind, see A. F. K. Organski and Jacek Kugler, *The War Ledger* (Chicago: University of Chicago Press, 1980), chap. 2. The measure in question was designed to estimate the performance of political systems in wartime or other situations of great stress. The index presented in this book, however, is specifically designed to capture the performance of political systems in times of peace.
3. Everett Hagen, for example, argues that substantial increases and eventual decreases in economic productivity have occurred repeatedly in advance of industrialization. Everett E. Hagen, *On the Theory of Social Change* (Homewood, Ill.: Dorsey, 1962).
4. See, for example, the set of relations presented by Samuel Huntington, *Political Order in Changing Societies* (New Haven: Yale University Press, 1968), 32.
5. For an extensive discussion of the ways scholars have approached the problem, see Charles Tilly, ed., *The Formation of National States in Western Europe* (Princeton: Princeton University Press, 1975), introduction and conclusion.
6. It is no accident that the scenario sketched here resembles that of G. Hardin's "The Tragedy of the Commons," *Science* 162 (1968): 1243-48.
7. Consider, for example, the ideas of the economic historian Alexander Gerschenkron regarding the variation in the European experience with economic development. He advances six propositions: "1. The more backward a country's economy, the more likely was its industrialization to start discontinuously as a sudden great spurt proceeding at a relatively high rate of growth of manufacturing output. 2. The more backward a country's economy, the more pronounced was the stress in its

industrialization on bigness of both plant and enterprise. 3. The more backward a country's economy, the greater was the stress upon producers' goods as against consumers' goods. 4. The more backward a country's economy, the heavier was the pressure upon the levels of consumption of the population. 5. The more backward a country's economy, the greater was the part played by special institutional factors designed to increase supply of capital to the nascent industries and, in addition, to provide them with less decentralized and better informed entrepreneurial guidance; the more backward the country, the more pronounced was the coerciveness and comprehensiveness of those factors. 6. The more backward a country, the less likely was its agriculture to play any active role by offering to the growing industries the advantages of an expanding industrial market based in turn on the rising productivity of agricultural labor." Alexander Gerschenkron, *Economic Backwardness in Historical Perspective* (Cambridge: Belknap Press, 1962), 353–54. If one applies these ideas to backward countries today, the prospects for currently underdeveloped countries are very poor precisely because modern economic technology has greatly increased the amount of capital investment required and the growth of population has greatly increased the share of total product that will need to be consumed. Even absolutist and totalitarian systems will find it increasingly difficult to meet requirements of resources for industrialization.

8. The relation between vital rates, economic development, and power has been stated in the model of the power transition: A. F. K. Organski, *World Politics*, 2d ed. (New York: Alfred A. Knopf, 1968), chap. 3. See also Organski and Kugler, *War Ledger*. An excellent illustration of the effects of the interaction of different rates of population and economic development between countries is given by Simon Kuznets: "In the period from 1834 to 1843, when the US was just entering its modern industrialization, it had a population of 16.7 million and a total product of $7.9 billion (in 1965 dollars). About the same time (1830–1840) France had a population of 33.9 million and a total product of some $8.2 billion (in the same prices). Thus the ratio of population in France to that in the United States was about 2.0; for total economic product it was slightly over 1.0. By 1965 the population of the United States was 195 million and its total product close to $700 billion, compared with a population of about 49 million and an economic product of $100 billion for France, with ratios of France to the United States of about one-quarter for population and one-seventh for total economic product. The comparison of the United States with the United Kingdom for two decades reveals a similar shift." Simon Kuznets, *Economic Growth of Nations: Total Output and Production Structure* (Cambridge: Belknap Press of Harvard University Press, 1971), 35. Kuznets goes on to indicate the implications of the shifts in question for the distribution of international power. "The significance of the association between high average growth rates, the wide absolute differences that can be generated, and rapid shifts of economic magnitude among nations lies in the possible connection between the shifts and strain producing attempts to modify political relations to correspond to the changed relation in economic magnitude, and hence possibly in economic and military power. The acceleration in the aggregate growth rates that produces acceleration of shifts in relative magnitude among nations may therefore cause acceleration in political adjustments and strains, and, under some conditions, in the frequency of conflicts in response to

recognized but disputed shifts in economic power" (p. 37). It is precisely the pattern and consequences of these shifts that the model of the "power transition" establishes.

9.   Among useful compendiums of population policies, we note three: B. Maxwell Stamper, *Population and Planning in Developing Nations: A Review of Sixty Development Plans for the 1970s* (New York: Population Council, 1977); Walter B. Watson, *Family Planning in the Developing World: A Review of Programs* (New York: Population Council, 1977); Dorothy Nortman and Ellen Hoffstatter, *Population and Family Planning Program*, 10th ed. (New York: Population Council, 1980).

10.   Alva Myrdal, *Nation and Family* (New York: Harper, 1941), 104–5. Quoted in Katherine Organski and A. F. K. Organski, *Population and World Power* (New York: Alfred A. Knopf, 1961), 189–90.

Chapter 1

1.   The initial conception of a characteristic demographic pattern is of uncertain origin, but its development and popularization are generally attributed to Thompson and Notestein, the latter being credited with the term "demographic transition." See Warren S. Thompson, "Population," *American Journal of Sociology* 34 (May 1929): 959–75, and Frank W. Notestein, "Population—The Long View," in *Food for the World* ed. T. W. Schultz, 36–57 (Chicago: University of Chicago Press, 1945).

2.   For the interested reader, we offer the following titles that provide past and current treatments of the work of "transition" theorists and also raise questions about the predictive and presumptive utility of this "theory" for currently developing nations. A. Coale, "The Demographic Transition," in *The Population Debate: Dimensions and Perspectives*, vol. 1 (New York: United Nations, 1975); D. Kirk, "A New Demographic Transition?" in *Rapid Population Growth* (Washington, D.C.: National Academy of Sciences, 1971); R. Freedman, "The Transition from High to Low Fertility: Challenge to Demographers," *Population Index* 31, 4 (October 1965): 417–29; M. Teitelbaum, "Relevance of Demographic Transition Theory for Developing Countries," *Science* 188 (2 May 1975): 420–25; F. W. Oechsli and D. Kirk, "Modernization and the Demographic Transition in Latin America and the Caribbean," *Economic Development and Cultural Change* 23, 3 (April 1975): 391–419. There are also many excellent journal articles discussing population changes addressed to the very knowledgeable general audience. See Ursula M. Cowgill, "The People of York: 1538-1812," *Scientific American* 222 (January 1970): 104; Carl E. Taylor, "Population Trends in an Indian Village," *Scientific American* 225 (July 1971): 17; William Langer, "Checks on Population Growth: 1750-1850," *Scientific American* 226 (February 1972): 92; Thomas Freyka, "The Prospects for a Stationary World Population," *Scientific American* 228 (March 1973): 15; Ronald Freedman and Bernard Berelson, "The Human Population," *Scientific American* 231 (September 1974): 30; Ansley J. Coale, "The History of Human Population," *Scientific American* 231 (September 1974): 40; Charles F. Westoff, "The Population of the Developed Countries," *Scientific*

American 231 (September 1974): 108; Paul Demeny, "The Populations of Under-developed Countries," *Scientific American* 231 (September 1974): 148.

3. The nomenclature used is Notestein's. Cf. Frank Notestein, "Population—The Long View."

4. The natural rate of increase (NRI) is the difference between crude birth and death rates.

5. In recent years a rich literature from the disciplines of sociology, psychology, and economics on "the value" of children and its relation to fertility has been emerging. A sampling from this material might usefully include: T. W. Schultz, "The Value of Children to Parents: An Economic Perspective," *Journal of Political Economy* 81 (1973): S2–S13; F. D. Bean et al., "Income and Supply and Demand for Children: Analysis of Wanted versus Unwanted Fertility," in *Research in Population Economics*, vol. 1 (Greenwich, Conn.: JAI Press, 1978); D. N. De Tray, "Child Quality and the Demand for Children," *Journal of Political Economy* 81 (1973): 570–95; L. W. Hoffman, "The Value of Children to Parents and the Decrease in Family Size," *Proceedings of the American Philosophical Society* 119 (1975): 430–38; J. T. Fawcett, ed., *The Satisfaction and Costs of Children: Theories, Concepts, Methods* (Honolulu: East-West Population Institute, 1972); F. Arnold et al., *The Value of Children: A Cross-National Study* (Honolulu: East-West Population Institute, 1975).

6. The issue has been defined as follows: "to assess the contributions that a nation makes to its power, we must ask four different questions: (1) How many people does a nation have? (2) How many of them now make, and in the future could make, a contribution to the achievement of national goals? (3) How motivated, skilled, and productive are they? (4) How successfully can their individual contributions be pooled in the joint pursuit of common national goals?" A. F. K. Organski, Bruce Bueno de Mesquita, and Alan Lamborn, "The Effective Population in International Politics," in *Governance and Population: The Governmental Implications of Population Change*, ed. Keir Nash, Commission on Population and Growth and the American Future, Research Reports (Washington, D.C.: Government Printing Office, 1972). One critical aspect of the connection between government and population is clearly suggested by question 4 above.

7. It is inexact to say that the process of deceleration had not been spotted earlier that the very late seventies. The coming deceleration had already been signaled in the middle sixties by Donald J. Bogue, who predicted the possibility of sharper declines than actually took place. Amy Ong Tsui and Bogue subsequently wrote: "Contrary to demographic predictions and official population forecasts, growth rates in the less developed countries appear to have begun a decline in recent years, considerably sooner than expected. The turning point seems to have occurred between 1970 and 1975, and appears to be progressing at an accelerating pace." Amy Ong Tsui and Donald J. Bogue, "Declining World Fertility: Trends, Causes, Implications," *Population Bulletin* 33, 4 (1978): 4; idem, "The End of the Population Explosion," *Public Interest* (Spring 1967). Even the critics of the overoptimistic fertility projection of Professor Bogue pointed to a 1963 United Nations projection that had both assumptions and projections indicating that substantial generalized decreases in fertility were to be expected. See Paul Demeny, "On the End of the Population Explosion," *Population and Development Review* 5, 1 (March 1979): 141–62, which disputes some of the claims made by Tsui

and Bogue, and the subsequent response by these authors in "A Reply to Paul Demeny's 'On the End of the Population Explosion,'" *Population and Development Review* 5, 3 (September 1979): 479–94, and a final rejoinder by Demeny in the same issue, pages 495–504. Despite such obvious disagreements within the demographic ranks on precise magnitudes of current and projected future fertility declines, there is a consensus that there have been overall declines within at least the past ten to fifteen years, with substantial declines in some countries and regions. See also W. Parker Mauldin, "Patterns in Fertility Decline in Developing Countries, 1950–1975," *Studies in Family Planning* 9, 4 (April 1978): 75–84, and W. Parker Mauldin and B. Berelson, "Conditions of Fertility Decline in Developing Countries, 1965–1975," *Studies in Family Planning* 9, 5 (May 1978): 90–147.

8. See Introduction, note 10.

9. As we noted above, in the preindustrial period in Europe vital rates were not uniformly high, as had previously been assumed, but fluctuated profoundly over time (almost, but not quite, as much as the decreases in the vital rates that accompanied economic development) and differed substantially across countries. It is difficult to pinpoint precisely why such fluctuations occurred. With regard to the demographic transition theory, a fundamental problem would arise if the sharp reduction in fertility were similar to the reductions in population growth that accompanied economic development in the current epoch. We would certainly hazard the guess that the answer to this question about fluctuations in vital rates should be in the negative. And we would also guess that the major difference between the two sets of decreases is that the decreases in population growth that accompany development are not reversible whereas decreases from the high rates recorded in the preindustrial epoch in Europe obviously were. We think the poor correlation between fertility, mortality, and socioeconomic change in preindustrial societies is due to the fact that effects of weak economic development on vital rates are also, by definition, very weak, and in such circumstances "other factors" supply the force driving vital rates up and down. In other words, in societies that live pretty much at subsistence levels and in which both mortality and fertility are high and the only significant international, national, or simply regional stimuli on vital rates are war, famine, outbreaks of pestilence, and natural disasters such as droughts, floods, or earthquakes, local conditions will play a correspondingly greater part in determining patterns of births and deaths. Important local conditions would include a long list: for example, local cultural patterns, bountiful harvests or food shortages at the local level, special usages or marriage customs in a particular village, the presence of a particularly determined or pious priest—all these factors and many more like them would affect birthrates in one locality as against another.

10. Paul Demeny, "Early Fertility Decline in Austria-Hungary: A Lesson in Demographic Transition," *Daedalus* (Spring 1968): 502.

11. Nathan Keyfitz, *Applied Mathematical Demography* (New York: John Wiley, 1977), 361.

12. Teitelbaum, "Relevance of Demographic Transition Theory for Developing Countries." It should be noted that Dr. Teitelbaum's article was in part a reply in a debate that took place at the Bucharest conference on population held in 1974 over the best way to deal with the immense population increases in the developing

world. Very briefly, at that conference one view held that the birth control efforts that had been backed by many of the developing countries' governments had not worked, at least in the sense that, quite obviously, they had not redirected fertility downward sufficiently to spark economic development, an event that would in turn have powerfully accelerated decrease in vital rates. The view that seemed to predominate at the conference was that the way to bring fertility down was to promote economic development. If one did that, the population problem would take care of itself.

It is our view that calls to abandon population planning programs, in whole or in part, under the argument that economic development will take care of the population problems of developing nations are clearly misleading. This is because the reason for the continuing population problem is precisely the persistent failure of all efforts at pushing the less developed world along the path toward economic development. Clearly developmental programs would require efforts and resources that did not seem to be available. And the relatively small investment in population planning, though insufficient to start development on its way, can surely be supplementary to any of the other moves being called for.

13. Geoffrey McNicoll, "Institutional Determinants of Fertility Change," *Population Development Review*, 441–62.

14. Demeny, "On the End of the Population Explosion."

15. Craig Bolton and J. William Leasure, "Evolution politique et baisse de la fécondite en Occident," *Population* 4, 5 (July/ October 1979): 825.

16. Kuznets, *Economic Growth of Nations*.

17. W. Parker Mauldin cites a number of estimates of Chinese birthrates ranging between fourteen and twenty-one per thousand and another estimate ranging between twenty-one and thirty-nine. "Patterns of Fertility Decline in Developing Countries, 1950–1975," 77. Chinese claims are now being taken quite seriously by non-Chinese scholars. There is no question that the estimates may contain considerable error and that the reporting system favors the overestimation of rates of decline. The interesting questions at present are how large the error will turn out to be and, of course, how long it will take before central authorities discover the major mechanisms that produce the errors in the system. We should realize that, in view of the estimates, the size of the error that can be tolerated is very large. If Chinese claims are accurate, the reduction in fertility in the People's Republic of China to levels associated with economic development is an incredible sociopolitical achievement and a clear exception to the rule.

18. A. F. K. Organski and Jacek Kugler, "Technical Report on National Estimates Project," unpublished manuscript, DARPA 1979.

19. A question of critical importance relating to the incredible achievement of the People's Republic of China in lowering fertility rates to reported levels is, of course, Can such levels be maintained unless socioeconomic development "catches up" with the modernization of their political system? We suspect that if the economy and the social structure do not modernize, present low fertility rates may not be sustainable and birthrates will tend to rise.

20. In some cases "refused" is the precise term. In an amusing incident, though it hardly seemed amusing at the time, one enthusiastic economic demographer in a United States government agency argued, with justifiable pride in the power of

economic variables, that politics had nothing to do with any reduction in birthrates in the less developed world. For example, if it were indeed true that a difference in birthrates existed between China and India (hard data on China were not then available), the reasons were rooted in income distribution. She did not pause to question what could have caused the difference in income distribution in the two systems. Incredibly, she did not see, or did not think worth considering, that the far-reaching differences in the penetration and effectiveness of the two political systems may have contributed a great deal to the income distribution of the two nations. The sharp, smooth decline in mortality and the slower but definite and profound decrease in birthrates (the Chinese *claim*, and the claim is now credited, an additional six-point drop in their crude birthrate) are a classic example of the behavior of vital rates under pressure from socioeconomic development. Only, in China, socioeconomic development had not, and political "development" had, taken place. It took a good deal of obtuseness to argue that social or economic factors or both could have been the entire cause. But such obtuseness comes naturally if one has been trained not to see what is in front of one's nose.

21. The point is perceptively observed by Demeny: "[The] claim that fertility declines for the rest of the century will be determined in the main by the strength of the family planning effort and their assumptions about the need for foreign assistance are better substantiated in situations in which the obstacles to rapid development are particularly great. China, which looms so large in aggregate world demographic indicators, could be an ideal example, and indeed is often cited as the most impressive country demonstration of family planning's success. But the example, of course, does not fit well into the frame of Bogue and Tsui's analysis. Clearly, foreign assistance played no role whatever in China's population success story, such as it may be. As to the vigor of China's family planning program, it was inseparably part—indeed, an appendage—of a comprehensive, not to mention socially "disruptive," institutional restructuring of Chinese society. Without that institutional transformation, the fertility decline that has occurred could hardly have taken place. This is not just because the institutions created were necessary for organizing and sustaining effective birth control services, but also, and probably primarily, because the institutional restructuring created the basis for programmatically supported group decisions favoring later marriage and lower fertility, as well as the probably indispensable social and administrative pressure to make such decisions stick.

"The other demographic giant, India, provides a much closer example of the conscious development by the government of a family planning program as an autonomous sector in its own right, with foreign assistance in an important supporting role. Unhappily, the 27-year history of that program also illustrates the severe limitations of such an approach." Paul Demeny, "On the End of the Population Explosion," 154.

22. It should be noted that we are not comparing the same periods in these three countries. In each case we wanted to take the hundred years immediately preceding the beginning of the industrial revolution. In England that date was 1750 (E. J. Hobsbawm, *Industry and Empire: From 1750 to the Present Day*, Pelican Economic History of Britain, vol. 3 [Baltimore: Penguin Books, 1976]), in France 1830, (Kuznets, *Economic Growth of Nations*, chap. 1, table 1) and in Germany about

1850 (ibid.). For Prussia data on vital rates were not available for a hundred years before the point of economic takeoff. That series begins in 1816.

23. David D. Bien, for example, in a recent study of the chancelleries of France under the ancien régime, points out that the sale of offices was a major source of indirect taxation that played an important role in supporting the ballooning costs of the French state in the eighteenth century. "The Secrétaires du Roi: Absolutism, Corps, and Privilege under the Ancien Régime," in *De l'ancien régime à la révolution française* (Göttingen: Vandenhoeck und Ruprecht, 1978).

24. This is clearly the dominant view among serious students of the question. See, for example, the magnificent book by Alexander Gerschenkron, *Economic Backwardness in Historical Perspective*, chap. 1 and pages 353–55. For an explicit statement of the relation between political and economic development where political development is treated as the *independent* variable, see Robert Holt and John Turner, *The Political Basis of Economic Development* (Princeton, N.J.: D. Van Nostrand, 1966), and the excellent essays by Gabriel Ardant, "Financial Policy and Economic Infrastructure of Modern States and Nations," and Rudolf Braun, "Taxation, Sociopolitical Structure and State Building, Great Britain and Brandenburg Prussia," in *The Formation of National States in Western Europe*, ed. Charles Tilly, 164–327 (Princeton: Princeton University Press, 1975).

25. Ibid.

Chapter 2

1. The theoretical literature dealing with different experiences of state making is immense, and summarizing it is extremely difficult. As a rule, for obvious reasons, very few attempts are made to view the entire trajectory of the developmental process. In the main, scholars seem to ask these questions: Why does the state structure begin to be built? What factors make for the increase in the rates of growth of the political system? What propels the process at the developed level? Some of the works influential in this chapter are: E. H. Carr, *Nationalism and After* (New York: Macmillan, 1977); Charles Tilly, *The Formation of National States in Western Europe* (Princeton: Princeton University Press, 1975); Perry Anderson, *Lineages of the Absolutist State* (London: New Left Books, 1974); Reinhardt Bendix, *Nation Building and Citizenship* (New York: Wiley, 1964); idem, *State and Society* (Berkeley: University of California Press, 1968); A. F. K. Organski, *The Stages of Political Development* (New York: Alfred A. Knopf, 1965); Granfranco Poggi, *The Development of the Modern State* (Stanford: Stanford University Press, 1978); Samuel P. Huntington, *Political Order in Changing Societies* (New Haven: Yale University Press, 1978); Barrington Moore, Jr., *Social Origins of Dictatorship and Democracy* (Boston: Beacon Press, 1966); E. J. Hobsbawn, *Industry and Empire* (Baltimore: Penguin Books, 1976).

2. For relatively short periods it is also possible for a religious or economic institution such as a religious order or a labor union to mobilize a mass population. Iran and Poland are two current examples of such events.

3. The strong connection between the expansion of the state system and war has long been attested by classic writers in the field of economics. See Adam Smith,

The Wealth of Nations (London: Cannon, 1904), vol. 2, book 5, chap. 3. See also J. Stuart Hull, *Principles of Public Economy* (London: Ashley, 1909), book 5, 788–880. For an excellent treatment of the subject, see also Samuel Finer, "State and Nation Building in Europe: The Role of the Military," and Gabriel Ardant, "Financial Policy and Economic Infrastructure of Modern States and Nations," both in *The Formation of National States in Western Europe*, ed. Charles Tilly (Princeton: Princeton University Press, 1975). Peacock and Wiseman, in an excellent treatment of the expansion of the public sector in the United Kingdom, suggest that war is a major mechanism in pushing up public expenditure and creates the conditions that help prevent expenditures (and revenues) from receding to prewar levels once the war is over. Their statement is entirely descriptive, but it makes the connection clear. See Alan T. Peacock and Jack Wiseman, *The Growth of Public Expenditure in the United Kingdom* (Princeton: Princeton University Press, 1961), chap. 4.

4.   One reads with sympathy the statement of two economists embarking on an exploration of the "reasons" for the expansion of the "state" or "public sectors" in the United Kingdom. "Finally, we do not base our discussion upon any all embracing theory of the state; our sole 'political' propositions are that governments like to spend more money, that citizens do not like to pay more taxes, and that governments need to pay some attention to the wishes of their citizens." The statement is congruent with the summary of the model for the growth of the state presented above. Peacock and Wiseman, *Growth of Public Expenditure*, xxiii.

5.   In short, it is the conflict between groups over available resources that fuels the growth of the state; and of course it is the success of ruling elites in obtaining sufficient compliance with their demands that makes this control over their societies credible.

6.   The English commercial elites, for example, obtained access to cabinet decision making almost immediately after the reform bill of 1832.

7.   For an early attempt to test this proposition empirically, see Youssef Cohen, Brian Brown, and A. F. K. Organski, "The Paradoxical Nature of State Making: The Violent Creation of Order," *American Political Science Review* 75 (December 1981): 901–9.

8.   To employ an appropriate demographic analogy, we may compare this situation to the differences between cross-sectional or "period" life tables, based on current mortality experience, and generational or "cohort" life tables. The commonly used period rates need not exactly replicate cohort experiences in order to yield useful insights into mortality dynamics. Similarly, our cross-sectional analysis need not correspond precisely to past experience to provide genuine insights into political and economic development.

Chapter 3

1.   When we speak of the expansion of the state and the political system, and of the consequent increase in the state's capacity to mobilize resources, we are really concerned with two systemic behaviors that account between them for most of the differences in the relative effectiveness of the political establishments of different

countries. The first is the depth of government penetration into the national society, and the other is the level of resources that governments are able to extract from their societies through political networks. These two behaviors are of course closely related.

Note that a measure of the penetration of society by a political elite would be almost ideally suited for the kind of estimation we wish to carry out here. After all, as we suggested in chapter 1, we argue that it is precisely by their intrusion into the lives of their citizens that governments affect reproductive behavior. The depth of government penetration, however, is still inaccessible to systematic measurement. Work tending to reverse this state of affairs is now in progress: experiments with measures of political penetration are currently being carried out in the National Estimates Project by the Center for Political Studies of the Institute for Social Research at the University of Michigan. The measures being examined relate to the performance, or lack of performance, of political systems in extracting resources from their societies. This research is nevertheless only in its initial stages. Thus both the models and the data perhaps best suited for our present purpose are for the moment unavailable. The indexes that are available, however, will serve as good proxies for the measure we need here.

2. Organski and Kugler, *War Ledger.*

3. Delbruck, cited by Horace Freeland Judson, *The Eighth Day of Creation* (New York: Simon and Schuster, 1979), 51.

4. The earliest models permitting the estimation of government contribution to intercountry differences in tax performance assumed that if governments collected less in taxes than other governments subject to similar economic and social circumstances, they did so in large part because they did not try hard enough and that governments that performed better did so because they did in fact try hard enough. "Will" was assumed to have a lot to do with government tax performance. Raja Chelliah, Hassel Baas, and Margaret Kelly, "Tax Ratios and Tax Effort in Developing Countries, 1969–1971," *International Monetary Fund Staff Papers* (May 1974), called their models measures of tax effort. It was these models that opened the way to attempts to measure the capacity of political systems. In later investigations, however, the concept of government performance as a function of personal character and will had to be discarded. Indeed, the opposite needed to be assumed. Organski and Kugler, *War Ledger;* A. F. K. Organski and Jacek Kugler, "Davids and Goliaths: Predicting the Outcomes of International Wars," *Comparative Political Studies* 11, 2 (July 1978): 141–80. For other early treatments of the problem see Jorgen Lotz and Elliot Morss, "Measuring 'Tax Effort' in Developing Countries," *International Monetary Fund Staff Papers* 14 (1967): 478–99; Roy Bahl, "A Regression Approach in Tax Effort and Tax Ratio Analysis," *International Monetary Fund Staff Papers* (November 1971): 570–610.

5. Organski and Kugler, "Davids and Goliaths."

6. At the time of this research, models of political capacity for developed countries had been developed, but data for the World War II period were not available. Thus, percentage of total product allocated to defense was used as a proxy for the share of GNP extracted by the government during the war. A good deal of evidence suggests that the values are very similar.

7. We should note at this point that some of the new research in this area seems to

confirm this very important point. J. Kugler and W. Domke, "Comparing the Strength of Nations," paper presented at the American Political Science Association meeting, New York City, November 1981.

8. As the reader will recall, 40 percent is the maximum share of the GNP developing countries are expected to extract, and 55 percent is the corresponding share for developed countries.

9. Mauldin and Berelson, "Conditions of Fertility Decline in Developing Countries, 1965–76," 99.

10. Data used is from World Bank, *Socio-Economic Data Bank*, updated in *World Tables* (1979). For details of problems of comparison, see Milton Gilbert and Irving Kravis, *An International Comparison of National Product and the Purchasing Power of Currencies* (Paris: OECD, 1954); Milton Gilbert et al., *Comparative National Products and Price Levels* (Paris: OECD, 1958); Wilfred Beckerman, *International Comparisons of Real Income* (Paris: OECD, 1966). For developing countries see Irving B. Kravis, Zoltan Kenessey, Alan Heston, and Robert Summers, *A System of International Comparisons of Gross Product and Purchasing Power* (Baltimore: Johns Hopkins University Press, 1975); Irving B. Kravis, Alan Heston, and Robert Summers, *International Comparisons of Real Product and Purchasing Power* (Baltimore: Johns Hopkins University Press, 1979).

11. *Adjusted mortality rates*

$SDA_{it} = ASMR_{it} \times ASP$

$ADJ.CDR_{it} = \Sigma_k SDA_{it}/\Sigma_k ASP$

where

k	= Age
i	= Nation
t	= Time
SDA	= Standardized number of deaths by age
ASMR	= Age-specific mortality rate (when unavailable, calculated using model life tables)
ASP	= Age-specific standard population (England, Wales, 1960)
ADJ.CDR	= Age-standardized crude death rates

12. *Adjusted fertility rates*

$ADJ.CBR_{it} = (PWP_{it}/PWSP)CBR_{it}$

where

PWP_{it}	= Percentage women 15–44 in national population
PWSP	= Percentage women 15–44 in standard population (England, Wales, 1960)
CBR	= Crude birthrate

Chapter 4

1. Cf chap. 1 of this volume.

2. We should note that the sample of nations we have used for the analysis is representative of the spectrum of nations in the international system. The sample includes ninety nations, forty-two of them analyzable for the whole period 1950–75.

The vast majority of nations in the sample fall in the "transitional" stage, only a few fall in the stage of "high potential growth," and the remainder are in the stage of "incipient decline" (see Appendix 2).

3. Even countries newly liberated from colonial rule went through a substantial period of state construction during the colonial period, as colonizers set up the minimal institutional framework necessary for them to rule, and again during the fight for liberation, when the rebellious colonials built the makeshift armies and parallel political bureaucracies essential to carry on the fight.

4. Data for Eastern European countries are now being collected. If fresh reanalysis of the connection between political development and vital rates seems warranted, it should be possible to attempt this in a few years, closing the gaps encountered in the present study.

5. See Appendix 1.

6. See Appendix 1.

Chapter 5

1. Huntington, *Political Order in Changing Societies*, 1.

Epilogue

1. "A population policy, . . . is a deliberate effort by a national government . . . to influence fertility, mortality, or migration, as opposed to those customs and institutions that may affect population size and composition but that were not designed to do so. For example, the institution of marriage influences the birthrate—among other ways—by discouraging childbearing among the unmarried, but marriage is not a population policy. The deliberate effort of the Nazi government to encourage illegitimacy, however, ranks as a population policy, since this effort was intended to increase the birthrate. Communist China's efforts to postpone the age of marriage must also be considered population policy if they were designed with an eye to reducing family size, but not if they were planned solely to free young men and women for work and study. The difference is one of intention and hence not always easy to ascertain.

Second, a policy envisages a change from what would otherwise have been. Makers of policy, looking into the future, foresee a discrepancy between what probably will occur and what they would like. Policy is designed, of course, to change the course of events. A major prerequisite, then, of successful policy planning is the accurate prediction of future population trends—a science that has not been notoriously successful in the past.

Finally, population policy is collective—adopted in the name of a group and enacted by its constituted authorities. Individuals and private organizations may recommend to their hearts' content, but only a government can put into effect a policy designed to influence the behavior of a whole community. Practically speaking, this means that modern population policy is national in scope and is planned and put into effect by national governments. Some claim that an international population policy is highly desirable, others that it is to be avoided at all costs. The argument is highly academic, however, because few matters touch as close to the heart of sovereignty as the right of a national group to decide the size and nature of its membership. It is a simple statement of fact to say that as long as national governments are the predominant holders of power—as they are today and as they are likely to be in the near future—the control of population will remain a national affair.

Population policy, then, is a deliberate effort by a national government to influence the demographic variables: fertility, mortality, and migration" (Organski and Organski, *Population and World Power*, 181–82).

2. Ronald Freedman and Bernard Berelson, "The Record of Family Planning Programs," *Studies in Family Planning* 7 (January 1976): 3–4. Freedman and Berelson provide a substantial list of sources where critical reviews of population planning are presented.

By way of illustration, these are among the critical commentaries: *Action Pack* (distributed by the World Population Year Secretariat of the UNFPA, 1974); Samir Amin, "Development Strategies and Population Policies: Underpopulation in Africa," in *Population-Education-Development in Africa South of the Sahara* (meeting of experts, Dakar, UNESCO Regional Office for Education in Africa, November-December 1971); Ahmed Bahri et al., "A New Approach to Population Research in Africa: Ideologies, Facts and Policies" (paper issued at the African Population Conference, Accra, December 1971); Judith Blake, "Demographic Science and the Redirection of Population Policy," in *Public Health and Population Change: Current Research Issues* ed. Mindel C. Sheps and Jeanne C. Ridley, 41–69 (Pittsburgh: University of Pittsburgh Press, 1965); Michael Carder and Robert Park, "Bombast in Bucharest: Report on the World Population Conference," *Science for the People* (January 1975), 17–19; Rick Casey, ed., "A Frustrated Consensus" (Report on the consultation on population policy cosponsored by the Canadian Inter-Church Project on Population and the Center of Concern, Montreal, October 1973); Kingsley Davis, "Population Policy: Will Current Programs Succeed?" *Science* 158 (10 November 1967): 730–39; Hardin, "Tragedy of the Commons"; Philip Hauser, "Family Planning and Population Programs: A Book Review Article," *Demography* 4 (1967): 397–414; idem, "Population: More Than Family Planning," *Journal of Medical Education* 44, 11, part 2 (November 1969): 20–29; W. T. Li, "Temporal and Spatial Analyses of Fertility Decline in Taiwan," *Population Studies* 27, 1 (March 1973): 97–104; Pierre Pradervand, "The Malthusian Man," *New Internationalist*, no. 15 (May 1974): 20–24, and Letter of Correction to Editor (9 September 1974); William Rich, "Smaller Families through Social and Economic Progress" (monograph no. 7, Overseas Development Council, January 1973); N. B. Ryder, "Realistic Pathways to Fertility Reduction in Developing Countries" (paper presented at the annual meeting of the Population Association of America, April 1974); Paul Singer, "Population Growth: The Role of the Developing World" (paper presented at the World Population Conference, in IUSSP Lecture Series on Population, Bucharest, 1974).

3. B. Berelson, "Romania's 1966 Anti-Abortion Decree: The Demographic Experience of the First Decade," *Population Studies* 33, no. 2 (July 1979): 209–22.

4. More than twenty years ago, Alexander Gerschenkron, in a seminal study, showed the relation between the level of available resources, the requirements

156   Notes to Page 128

imposed on the amount of resources needed, the moment at which economic development is begun, the rise in population, and the centralization of political power and repression. Although during the period 1900–1945 a highly decentralized process could produce the conditions for development in England for socioeconomic development in a relatively nonviolent manner, in Russia direct state intervention was probably the only instrument capable of accumulating the capital needed for industrialization. *Economic Backwardness in Historical Perspective.*

5. Organski, *World Politics.*

Index

Abortion, 13, 30, 124, 125
Africa, 22, 26, 51, 89
Age structure: changes in, and development, 20; differences in, and crude vital rates, 82–84, 112
Agricultural wealth, and taxation, 71
Algeria, 133, 140
Angola, 133
Argentina, 93
Asia, 22, 26, 54, 89
Australia, 133
Austria, 37, 133

Bangladesh, 32
Belgium, 133
Berelson, Bernard: on family planning programs, 120–21; and Rumania study, 125–26
Birth control. *See* Contraceptives; Family planning programs
Birthrates, *See* Fertility rates
Bolivia, 133
Brazil, 93, 128, 133, 140
Bureaucracies: and political expansion, 45–51, 74, 110, 114
Burundi, 133, 140

Cameroon, 133, 140
Canada, 133
Central African Empire, 133, 141
Chad, 133
Children, costs of having, 30
Chile, 133
China, People's Republic of, 2–3; fertility rate in, 6–7, 32, 122–23, 148–49nn. 17–21; political effectiveness of, 11, 35–38, 57, 58; as world power, 128–29

Coale–Demeny model life tables, 83–84
Colombia, 133
Communist countries: excluded from study, 89, 93; fertility rate in, 32, 129; political parties in, 54; political versus socioeconomic development of, 57–58
Congo, 133
Contraceptives, 13, 124, 125
Costa Rica, 133, 141; age pyramid for, 21 illus.
Cyprus, 55
Czechoslovakia, 93; population policy of, 13

Death rates. *See* Mortality rates
Delbruck, Max, 64
Demeny, Paul, 25
Democracies: and extractive capacity, 70; political parties in, 53–54
Demographic transition theory, 17–28, 33, 87; methodology of, 20–22, 56–57, 88; objections to, 20–28, 34–35, 108; outlined, 17–20, 107
Denmark, 133
Development: in demographic transition theory, 17–27; and extractive capacity, 48–49, 55–56, 68–70, 75; and fertility rates, 59–61, 94–98, 102–4, 113; groupings relating to, 89–94; modern and premodern compared, 8–11, 22–23, 38–43, 57–58, 126; and mortality rates, 59–61, 98–104, 113–14; and political expansion process, 45–59, 110–11; prospects for, in developing world, 10–13, 127–29, 143n.7, 155n.4; and

157